MW00911817

Chocolate Boy
The Philosophy of One Child
Of South Sudan

By Antoni Bazia
(as told to Ann B. Smith)

Bazia

To

Chocolate Boy
The Philosophy of One Child of South Sudan
Written by Antoni Bazia
(as told to Ann B. Smith)

About Antoni Bazia: Born on Christmas Day, 1971, 12 years before the outbreak of the Second Civil War in Sudan, Antoni Bazia grew up in relative affluence and physical security because his *Daddy*, Henry Bazia, was not only chief of the Lou tribe, but also an important official of the Arabic government in Khartoum. Although he was a Christian and often promoted the causes of the African peoples who dominated the south of Sudan, Henry Bazia was respected and valued by the Islamic leadership, and his children grew up *under his umbrella*.

Antoni, or Toni, as his family called him, never had to flee for his life, see his family massacred, or his home burned to the ground as did *The Lost Boys* whom he would later support and advise in the U.S.A., Canada, and the U.K. His childhood had different challenges, character-building exercises which would give him strength and clarify a personal philosophy which can be followed by any child who wants a life of purpose and deep spiritual rewards. This book was written to share his inspiration and common sense not only with you, the children of South Sudan, to whom he dedicates this book and his life, but the children of the world.

About Ann B. Smith: As a former English teacher from New Hampshire, Ann B. Smith retired to Portland, Maine in 2009 where she took long walks, attended the symphony, and volunteered to teach English as a Second Language to refugees, many of whom were from Africa. Three years later, Antoni Bazia enrolled in her class, told her his dreams for supporting his people, and asked for her help. She has been working with him ever since because she "always wanted to be part of something *big*!" and this is *her* chance to fulfill her childhood dream.

3

Chapter One: God's Plan

The hardest thing about writing this book was deciding where to begin. I have been told that the simplest plan is to begin at the beginning, but my beginning was the moment when I was first conceived in my mother's womb, and before that, I was, according to what I believe, only a thought in the mind of God. That is how every one of us begins.

You may have heard of this belief before. Many people already believe it, and the numbers are growing, day by day, or you may think this sounds incredibly arrogant. How, you ask, can a being who is only one of billions on this planet now think of himself as part of God's plan? But I believe that I am. And that you are, as well. Again, and I know I am repeating myself, but this is an important point, perhaps the most important: we are all part of God's plan.

Now I suppose your next question is "What is God's plan?" I think you are right to ask, but I cannot answer that question. I don't know what His plan is. It is just too big for me to understand. After all, if everyone of us is part of this plan, then the plan is very very complicated indeed.

I have been told that when numbers get up into the millions, we human beings cannot really wrap our tiny brains around such concepts. I have been an automobile mechanic most of my life and as a result, I know a lot about cars. I have never counted, but I would guess that cars have parts that number into the hundreds, maybe even a thousand, and I can think about those parts one at a time, or even several parts at a time when I think about how they work together in a group, like the parts of the braking system that make the car stop, but if I then try to add in the transmission, and the engine, and, well, I think you can see how difficult it gets. When I try to think about the whole car and all of its parts working together, I cannot do more than jump from thinking about one system to another. I cannot really think about the whole car at once. So as a human being, I am very very limited in my understanding of a plan that has parts that number into the billions.

In fact, it's even more complicated than that. God's plan doesn't just exist for every person living on this planet right now; it exists for every person who has ever lived or will ever live. God's plan has been going on since the beginning of time and it will continue long after you and I and all of the people we know are gone. If this makes you sad, it shouldn't. The end of life, death, is part of God's plan, too, just as much as the beginning.

But I want to talk more about what most people think when someone like me says he believes he is a part of God's plan. They seem to react as if they think I am trying to make myself important. They say things like, "Who do you think you are?" and "What could you ever do to change the world so that it will be closer to God's plan?" Sometimes they are even a little frightened by my belief, as if they expect me to start pushing them to change. Am I going to try to convince them to sell everything they have and go sit on a mountain top somewhere and wait for the rest of God's plan to unfold? Or will I try to drag them into a place of religious worship? Notice I don't say a church or a temple or a mosque. They often want to know which of those I attend; my answer is all of them. Then they ask which one teaches what I believe; my answer again is *all of them*, but at the same time, *none of them*. Later, I will try to explain that a little more completely, but for now, all you need to know is that I value all religious beliefs, and I respect and honor all religious faiths and the good works they do, but I don't believe that any one of them has all of the answers for having a good life and for, yes, following God's plan. Again, we are back to talking about a plan that involves billions, or trillions, or maybe octillions of human souls, not just mine.

So let me assume you are with me at this point in my belief. You understand that I think I came into this life to fulfill some part of God's plan. So did you. So did your parents and so did the family that lives next door to you and the next people down the street and on and on until you have included every human being for of all time. And this huge plan is in the mind of God. We cannot really understand it. To put it very bluntly, you may be thinking, "Well, so what? Maybe I am part of this plan, but I don't know what the plan is, let alone my part. So why do I need to think about this at all? If all of us are part of God's plan, then His plan should just roll along and work itself out without any understanding or effort on our parts. After all, God is, by definition, all powerful. We are just the parts of this big plan, like the parts of the car. Doesn't He just get in and drive His plan away? He doesn't need our understanding or our conscious participation, does He?"

Ah, but He does. We aren't His tools or bits of machinery. We are human beings. We have minds, we have feelings, we have our own needs and desires, and we make choices of our own. And God doesn't control that. We have something called free will, which is the ability to choose to follow or not to follow God's plan. In fact, when we first came into the world, for a long time while we were growing from little babies into little children and then getting bigger and bigger and learning more about ourselves and the world around us and how it works, we were mostly busy just taking care of that business. We were still a part of God's plan, but unless we were very fortunate and were born into a family or situation where this sense of purpose was explained to us and shown to us by the examples of people around us, we tend to keep the focus on ourselves. We have to focus on gaining control of our bodies so that we can walk and talk and run and climb a tree or jump out of the way when we are in danger. We have to become independent, feeding ourselves and getting dressed, keeping ourselves clean and healthy. We have to learn how to get along with others, not only in our own families, but outside of the house, at school and on the playground. We have to go to school and learn to read and write and how numbers work so we can keep the progress of civilization going. All of that learning and growing and changing is necessary so we can survive and live long enough to begin to seek our happiness.

Why am I talking about happiness now? I was talking to you first about God's plan.
What has your happiness or mine got to do with God's plan?

I'm going to tell you a secret. Your happiness is a part of God's plan. It is one of the ways He communicates with you. And it is a very important way you learn how to have a good life, a life which allows you to fulfill your part in God's plan.

If you are old enough to read this book, you know what real happiness is. You know it is the feeling that you get when you have chosen well. It isn't just the feeling of being safe and well fed. It's much bigger than that. It isn't the feeling you get on a special day when you open a box and there are the new shoes that you have been wanting for weeks, even months. They are now yours and they fit. You put them on and jump around the room. And that gives you pleasure for a while.

But maybe in a few days you will accidentally step in a dirty puddle and your new shoes will get wet and messy. They won't look so great anymore and wearing them may not give you the same kind of pleasure. You are still glad you have them, but you may have also seen a great looking jacket, red or bright blue or white with your favorite team's logo and name on it, and now you are hoping to get that. And if you do, the cycle of pleasure will start again. You will feel satisfied with this new thing, but that feeling isn't real happiness. And it doesn't last.

Real happiness is not getting something: it is giving something. It goes in the opposite direction from pleasure, outward toward some other being or person, making his or her existence better, but then, it circles back to you with a feeling that is so powerful that the pleasure of just receiving what you want can't compare. And there is an excellent reason why this is so; it's because you have chosen well. You have chosen to follow God's plan, and He is rewarding you with that quiet feeling of joy inside you.

I'd like you to think about the last time you did something for someone else. Maybe you helped a younger person, your baby brother or sister, tie a shoe. Or you saw an older lady struggling to open a door while her arms were full of packages, and you opened it for her. Or you drew a picture of the sun shining on some flowers and you gave this picture to your mother. She put it up on the wall and you both stood and looked at it. You could have gotten that special happiness because you noticed someone standing around with a long face who looked upset, and you stopped in your busy life and said, "Hi, what's up? Can I help?" Maybe you couldn't really solve his problem, but you did listen and you expressed your concern and that person went on his way feeling a little less burdened with his own despair because of your attention.

What you give to other people doesn't have to be big like a huge sum of money which leaves you not being able to pay your own bills. You also don't have to wave your gift to another around in public like you're showing off. In fact, that's probably going to have a negative effect on your happiness because inside yourself, in your soul, the part where God is connected to all of us, you know you weren't really giving. You were really thinking about yourself and what you could get, like the admiration of others for your good deed.

I am going to appear to change the subject here, but stay with me. I want to talk about rich people and poor people. I have met a lot of both kinds of people in my travels around the world, and I can tell you one thing for sure. In terms of happiness, there is absolutely no connection between being rich or being poor. I have met millionaires who were miserable and paupers who woke up smiling every day. I have also met people with very little money who used whatever they had to make others happy, and I have seen people with much in the way of material wealth who made themselves very very unhappy by focusing constantly on what they wanted and what they weren't getting. Happiness is a result of your attitude toward your place in the world and the choices you make about your behavior.

I want to talk about the attitude part first because I think it was one of the first pieces of wisdom I received from watching other people when I was a very young child. If you look at my baby picture which is on the front of this book, you see a really happy baby. I was obviously well fed and well cared for. My smile spreads across my whole face. My eyes almost sparkle with my eagerness to look at and listen to the world around me. And being the second child, I did just that.

My parents celebrated my birth, of course, but it was my Daddy's father, my Grandpop, who was especially happy to see me. The first time he saw me, he said I was going to be more like him than I would be like my Daddy. He called me his little *chocolate boy* because my skin was same color as milk chocolate. He also dedicated himself to encouraging my eagerness to observe the world and think about it. He was a strong influence and a great blessing in my life.

I was the second child in a family of what would be four children, but I best remember watching my older brother, Bazia (which is also the name of our traditional chief and therefore often given to the oldest son), who was four years older than me and my younger sister, Ireni, younger by two years, as I recall.   My younger brother, Batista, was so much younger than I as to be almost a stranger for a long time. It is, perhaps, the advantage of being the second child that I could learn from my older brother's mistakes, but given my father's attitude toward discipline, we were all forced to learn from each other's mistakes. Some of us did and some of us didn't.

In most families, if a child breaks a rule or causes trouble, only that child is punished while his brothers and sisters stand by and watch, rejoicing in their good fortune. But my father, perhaps because of something he had learned in the military, always punished all of us whenever one of us misbehaved. He said that way no one of us would make that same mistake a second time. He said it would save time! We would all remember the punishment and we would all remember why it was done. As for the punishment, it was always the same, and no, he didn't beat us. But I will talk about that more in a minute. It was an effective but not cruel punishment: it hurt enough that we could remember but it didn't make us fearful or nervous like children who are hit. Our Daddy was fair. He made a point of explaining each time what one of us had done wrong and how important it was that a parent teach his children how to behave, how to tell the right behavior from the wrong. He said this every time, that it was not to be mean or make us feel like bad people. The punishment was to teach us.

But my brother and my sister didn't seem to hear him. They often appeared to be thinking about their own thoughts or their feelings whenever our Daddy was explaining this to them. Young Bazia, for so the servants called him, would bring his eyebrows down and his mouth would form a snarl. He tried to keep this fierce expression on his face throughout our Daddy's talking and then through the punishment. I often wondered if his face hurt when the punishment was over. Ireni would cry a little and her mouth would tremble as if she were afraid, although I knew this was just an act she did to avoid the punishment. My Daddy didn't believe her either. He ignored the sniffing and trembling lips and continued to explain right up to when the punishment began.

And now I will tell you what that was. The punishment was always the same, although as you got older, it got a little harder. We would all kneel on the floor in a line but not close together. We had to be far enough apart that when we stretched our arms out straight, we couldn't touch each other. Then our Daddy would tell us to open our hands, palms up, and he would put a brick in each hand. As we got bigger, we boys got two bricks in each hand. Then the punishment began. We had to hold the bricks up with our arms out straight from our bodies and not let them drop

11

back down until our Daddy said we could. Sometimes, if the bad behavior was not very bad, it would be only for fifteen minutes. Sometimes, if the behavior was very very bad, it could be for an hour, but never longer than that.

Now if you grew up in a house where you were beaten when you were bad, you might not think this was a very hard punishment. But it was. At first you were just a little uncomfortable, but after a while, your shoulders and arms would start to ache and ache and you wanted to let your arms fall down, but you knew if you did, you would have to start the punishment all over again from the beginning, and that was not a good thing at all. At the same time, your knees would begin to hurt from holding you up and you would wonder if they were turning black and blue from kneeling so long. But for me, the worst part was that I would get bored. I would watch my brother to see if he let his fierce expression slip, but if he did, it was only for a second, and he would put it back on again like a mask. My sister had usually given up with the sniffing and crying by this time, but she did keep her lower lip poked out in a pout. Snarling and frowning weren't for Ireni; she was very proud of her looks and was afraid that frowning would make her get wrinkles before it was her time.

When the punishment ended, it was important that we didn't drop the bricks on the floor. We had to set them down gently and get up and leave the room. My brother always stomped out, making as much of a scene as he could, but my sister also created a lot of noise by wailing and crying. I would put the bricks down, get up and dust off my knees, and walk out of the room like nothing much had happened. I would go to my room, pick out a clean outfit, take a shower, and change my clothes. Somehow for me, changing into a nice clean outfit always seemed like a new beginning to a new part of the day. I could hear my

12

brother stomping around his room and occasionally throwing something on the floor; my sister was still wailing that one of her arms felt like it was broken. I would sit in the chair in my room by the window and watch the gardener who was weeding or replanting a flower bed outside. I usually wondered why my siblings were wasting so much energy complaining about something that Daddy had to do because he loved us. By now, the ache in my arms was fading, probably because of the hot shower and a little rest.

These punishments usually happened in the afternoon, an hour or two before supper.
I remember the first time I was punished, not because of the punishment itself or what one of us (it could have been me!) had done to get punished, but because when supper time came, I went into the dining room and sat in my place just like I always did. Both my parents were there, but not my brother or my sister. (Batista, the youngest, was still in the nursery.) "What are you doing here, Toni?" they said.

"Was I told not to come to supper? " I asked politely. I couldn't remember that being part of the punishment, but maybe I missed something.

"No," said my Daddy, "but your brother and sister never eat after a punishment. I think," he said, glancing at my mother with half a smile, "they are mad and punishing us."

My mother smiled and shook her head as I looked at each of them.

"I don't see how their missing supper is a way to punish you," I said. My Daddy nodded and began to eat. It was an excellent meal.

So this is what I mean about attitude. I watched my brother and my sister, and later from time to time, my younger brother, do all the same silly things. It was as if they were determined to make any bad situation they got into worse. My older brother, for example, might accidentally bump into the corner of a table on his way through a room. He would cry out and turn swiftly and then kick the table leg as hard as he could to show his displeasure. He usually ended up hurting his foot that way as well.

And my sister watched him and copied everything he did. She might add her own little bit of personality to the fit of temper, like raising her hands in the air when she shrieked or saying, "oooh, ooh, ouch!" when she kicked the table leg, but she was really just copying him.

When other children came to the house, especially those a little older than us, my brother and sister would follow them around like little puppies and copy every silly thing they did. It was as if they never had a thought about what they themselves really wanted to do, except to be like everybody else, no matter what that meant.

My Daddy watched them, too. One time, when my brother had been playing like this for over an hour with two boys who often came to visit, my father pulled him aside. "Do you think these boys are better than you? " Daddy said.

"Better?" my brother didn't seem to understand the question.

"Yes, better, " said Daddy. "Because you do everything they do in just the same way."

"I think they're cool, " my brother said, "and I want them

14

to be my friends."

"But you are my son, " said Daddy. "You are the son of the chief of the Lou. Their father isn't a chief. You don't need to worry about winning their friendship. They already want yours."

My brother stood there in front of Daddy, shifting awkwardly from one foot to the other. He kept glancing at his two friends who were now heading toward the back of the house and the kitchen. They kept looking back at him, too, but they weren't slowing down.

"Can I go now, Daddy?" my brother said.

"In a minute," Daddy said. "You need to understand what it means to be the son of the chief. You are a special person. You are a lucky person. You are growing up under my umbrella and while you are living under my umbrella, you can do pretty much what you want to do, as long as you don't break any of my rules. Do you understand what that means, my son? It means that all you have to be is you."

Young Bazia nodded his head quickly, but I knew he didn't understand; he just wanted to get back to following his friends around like a puppy dog. I understood my Daddy however. I was really happy to hear him say this because I didn't want to be anybody's little puppy. I already knew who I wanted to be. I wanted to be me. And now I had my Daddy's permission.

Chapter Two: You Are Not My Child

It was shortly after this incident with the punishment and my appearance at the supper table that my mother began to say to me, "You are not my child." My brother and sister seemed to like hearing her say this. They would always look carefully at me, studying my reaction, hoping that I felt hurt or angry, I think, but I had for some time been careful to conceal my emotions from them and keep a calm expression. Besides, having looked carefully at my two siblings, who were obviously normal predictable children, the kind my mother liked, I wasn't all that sure that "being her child" was the best thing to be.

She said this often, her head tilted on one side in puzzlement, and I always responded politely, "That's ok." I rather liked being thought of as different from my siblings; after all, when I thought back to my Daddy's advice to my brother, if I was different, it probably meant that I was being me, not some copy of my brother or a neighbor or even my Daddy. I had also learned by that time that being different was not automatically bad, and that not every comment about me (or anyone else for that matter) was a judgment or needed to get an emotional reaction. I had learned early to listen and then to think about what was said. And after the thinking, came the deciding: did I have to take some kind of action about what was said? Usually, the answer to that question was no. It wasn't necessary to take everything personally, as a reflection or judgement upon me. In fact, quite often, what people said was a revelation of *their* inner thoughts or feelings; it was a reflection of what *they* were thinking, not what they saw in me. This is a very important thing for you to know and understand about this chocolate boy's philosophy, and knowing it will save you much pain. When others judge you, they are voicing their opinions, and opinions are not necessarily correct or fair. It's your opinion that matters the most!

There was, however, one of my Daddy's rules about our

family and how we lived that bothered me a lot because it didn't seem to fit with his advice to my brother when he told him to be him, that it wasn't necessary to be like anyone else. This inconsistency always occurred on Sunday mornings when the entire family went to the local Christian church together. My Daddy insisted that all of us children had to dress alike, like we were wearing uniforms. But this seemed inconsistent from a man who wanted each of us to be ourselves.

Looking back, I think, just like being punished all together for one person's sin, this was something from my Daddy's military experience. He did have a very orderly mind, so dressing his children for church in what amounted to a weekly uniform made sense. A parade of children, eventually all four of us, the family of the tribal chief, Henry Bazia, was also a display of his wealth, power, and the unity of this family. To see this group of future tribal leaders line up by height and stand all together next to their parents in the church pew must have been very reassuring to the people of the Lou. Everyone could see that the Bazia family was proper and correct: we were all in place and we were all the same. God was in His Heaven and all was right with the world.

Preparation for this weekly ritual actually began Saturday evening when we were told at the supper table what we should wear the following day. Sometimes it was navy blue suits and white shirts for the boys and a navy blue skirt and white blouse for the girl. Or perhaps this week, grey flannel pants and pinstriped blazers for the boys with cream-colored shirts and red ties, while Ireni wore a grey skirt, grey sweater, and a cream-colored blouse with a red bow tied under the collar?

There were other outfits; after all, we were an affluent

17

family. Our preparation on Sunday morning was always the same: we each took a shower, engaged in personal grooming, and then put on the outfit for that day. When we left the house and got into the chauffered car for our drive to the church, we would all look the same. And, of course, we would be right on time.

But as I grew older and became more confident of the wisdom of being myself, I decided to test this uniformity because it seemed to me that a rule that insisted on such consistency of dress was not allowing each one of us to be ourselves, and I had begun to enjoy the luxury of being me. I was now nine years old, and I was very different from all of my siblings. I was always quiet and controlled, polite and well-behaved. I didn't like to get dirty as they did when they played rough and tumble games outside. In fact, I was so fastidious that I showered and changed my clothes as often as three times in one day, especially if we had guests or I had an opportunity to sit and talk with my Daddy.

When other families came to visit, my brothers and sisters ran off with the other children in little packs, noisy and boisterous and often fighting. I stayed with the adults and sat quietly listening to their conversations. After a while, an adult would notice me and gesture for me to come sit with him or her. "Tell me what you think, Toni," this grownup would ask, and I would answer and we would talk some more. These people who talked with me were often amazed at what I had to say about life in the village or political problems in our city, but as often as I could, I sat and talked with my Daddy so I had learned more than most children my age. I knew I was different, that I was not my mother's child, and after a while, the idea that each Sunday I should dress up just like all the other children was not only disturbing, it was somehow humiliating. So I finally developed a strategy to make one Sunday morning different from all the rest.

I began by selecting an outfit one Saturday night which was completely different from the rest of my brothers and sisters. I hid it carefully under the blankets of my bed so that none of them would see it and tattle on me. One of the disadvantages of group punishment was that my siblings tended to watch each other fiercely for signs of potential disobedience. After all, if you are going to get punished whether you had a part in the behavior or not, you might as well rat out your brother or sister before the crime was committed.

On Sunday morning I executed the second part of my plan. I stalled taking my shower so that I would be the last one in the bathroom. I pretended to be too exhausted to get out of bed. When my brother yelled, "Hey, Toni, it's your turn," I rolled over and moaned that he should go next.

"No, no, " I said to my sisters, "You go next. I'm too tired. I don't mind. I just want to get a little more sleep." So I managed to make my shower the last one, and at the very last possible moment, I dashed into the bathroom, showered, and dressed. I didn't leave the bathroom until I heard the others going outside to get in the car. I waited until I heard my Daddy calling, "Where's Toni?"

"I'm coming, I coming," I cried as I headed out the front door and took my usual place in line.

There was a moment of stunned silence as everyone looked at me. "But, Toni," my mother said, "You aren't dressed like everybody else."

I looked down at my clothes and then at my brothers and

19

sisters in amazement. I did this very slowly, as if I were as surprised and bewildered by this turn of events as they all were. I made sure that I took as much time to do this as I could, assuring myself of more time to secure my goal. I knew how important punctuality was to my Daddy.

"I guess," I said, as innocently as I could, "I better go back in and change."

My parents looked at each other in silence for a moment, and then Daddy said, "No, I guess we'd better all just go. It wouldn't do to be late."

And so we left. We rode to the church in the car as we always did, got out, and marched inside in a straight line, first my parents, and then all four of us (for there were four children by then) neatly arranged by age and height. It gave me a certain satisfaction to look around at the congregation and see the shocked looks on some of the villagers' faces as each of them noticed that one boy was different from all the rest. It was a moment that I would never forget, but I also knew my Daddy wouldn't forget it either.

Every act has consequences, I knew, and this successful act of defiance was no exception. During the week that followed, there was no immediate reaction and no punishment for my behavior. I think I would have been able to relax if there had been a punishment, but nothing was said or done. I knew something was in the works because my mother and father were often seen in conversation, but when I got close enough to listen, they would stop talking and move away from me. I was convinced that these conferences must involve me because of the way they both looked at me.
They appeared to be studying me, much as I regularly

studied them and my brothers and sister.

By Friday of that week, I was considering whether I should make a new plan for the upcoming Sunday, but when I came home from school, the house was in an uproar. My siblings who regularly dashed away from school ahead of me and down the street like they were running for their lives were now running around the house from room to room, yelling and calling to each other, "Toni's being sent away! Toni's leaving!" Some of the servants were waving their hands in the air and shouting to each other remarks like "I can't believe it! " or "It's going to be terrible for him to stay with a poor family! How will he get along?"

I walked into the house and stood in the doorway. Everyone stopped yelling and running around for a moment and stared at me. Then, all together, they announced, "You are being sent away!" and the craziness started all over again.

"Who said? " I asked.

The head kitchen maid, a large and comfortable sort of woman, looked very concerned.

"Your mother told me, " she replied.

Then my older brother piped up, "Daddy told me. I asked him why he hadn't punished us for you wearing the wrong clothes last Sunday, and he told me that this was an *exceptional* situation." Bazia bore down on the word exceptional and rolled his eyes in dramatic disbelief.

"I'll bet you won't stay where they send you, " Ireni said. "I wouldn't stay. I'd rather die than stay in a village with poor people. I'd run away. I'd run away into the bush and then I'd get eaten by lions and everybody would be sorry!" Then she burst into tears and ran out of the room.

The head maid shook her head and then spoke again, "Your parents are waiting for you in the living room. You'd better go in there right now. Maybe they'll change their minds." As she finished speaking, the two maids who were standing nearby began to wail. They put their apron skirts over their faces and then they, too, ran down the hall after my sister.

I walked the other way and went into the living room. None of my siblings or any servants were there. My small brown leather suitcase was standing on the floor near my mother's feet. It looked packed.

There was a small wooden chair across from where my parents were sitting together on the couch. My mother indicated by pointing with her hand that this chair was for me, and I should go sit down in it. Obediently, I sat.

"Toni," my Daddy said, " you are going to go away for a little while." I had no idea how to respond, so I just smiled and nodded. I had learned at an early age to think before I spoke or acted; smiling and nodding were excellent ways to stall. If you did this, you committed yourself to nothing but listening, and you had plenty of time to think.

"This is not to punish you for last Sunday, " my Daddy went on, "but I do want you to know that both your mother and I are aware that what you did to get ready for church was not an accident."

I didn't smile or nod this time. My chair felt very uncomfortable all of a sudden.

"I have packed a few of your clothes for this," my mother paused in thought, and
then said, "little trip, but I may send more in a couple days. You won't need all your clothes, however. In fact," my mother looked at Daddy for his thoughts, and my father nodded, "it might be best if you take very little."

"How long will I be gone?" I asked. I kept my voice steady, but my heart was pounding somewhat fiercely in my chest.

"He doesn't want to know where he is going, " my mother said to my father. They looked at each other again, and then, Daddy shrugged in puzzlement before he turned back to me.

"At least a month," Daddy said.

"Will I still go to school?" I asked. There were at least ten days left before the summer vacation began.

"No," said Daddy, "the school there is already closed. You will be learning other kinds of lessons. Take your suitcase and come with us."

My parents rose from the couch and I followed them out into the front yard. The car was parked in front, and our chauffeur was standing at attention by the back door, ready to help my parents and me get in. My brothers and sister were standing nearby. They were all wearing very similar expressions. Despite all the yelling and crying and hullabaloo of only a few minutes ago, they were now smiling with intense satisfaction.

"Goodbye, Toni, " they said in chorus. "Maybe we'll see

you later!"

The driver opened the door and I got into the car after my mother. Daddy got in behind me, the door was closed, and we drove away. As it was the height of the rainy season, the Sudanese landscape was lush and green. I stared out the window at fields knee-deep in long grasses and an occasional tree overgrown with vines. Daddy spoke only one word to the chauffeur when he got in. It was the name of a little village I had seen on a map, south and west of Wau. Wherever we were going, it was a new place to me. I cannot deny that I was perhaps a little nervous, but I was also thinking that a new place was an opportunity for new experiences and new challenges. My siblings shouldn't smile in that superior way; I was the lucky one. I was going to find out more about another world, one which would be very different, I was sure, than the one I already knew.

The drive took about two hours; obviously, walking home was not an option, I thought. I also noticed that we passed through only one other village on the way. That one was very small and primitive. It had one concrete building in the center of a cluster of grass huts. It was the only permanent structure. It had one gas pump in front and a sign advertising beer. The other buildings were makeshift shacks of grass and thatch, easily destroyed by fire or wind. I also noticed that despite the gas pump, there were no automobiles in that village. This disappointed me as I already loved automobiles, even the miserable old wrecks that were often found abandoned in villages like this one.

As we traveled down the road, I began to doze a little. At one point, I slipped sideways toward my mother, but caught myself and jerked upright. I didn't want to fall asleep like a little boy. At nine, I considered myself well on the way to manhood, far beyond the childish behavior of falling asleep in the car and tipping into my mother's lap. I pulled myself up straight and stared down the road. The hot sun of late afternoon was causing shimmering mirages like pools of silver water to rise above the sandy surface. My Daddy took out his handkerchief and wiped the sweat from his forehead. My mother waved her hand in front of her face, fanning herself. Nobody said a word.

Occasionally we had to stop for people or animals crossing the road. Once, a herd of cattle, about thirty or forty, marched right in front of us, driven by a boy with a long stick. Their hooves stirred up the dust and it blew into the windows of our car, making all of us wipe our eyes and cough. Our chauffeur honked indignantly, but the boy and his cows only looked at us with dull expressions as they plodded to the other side.

It was getting dark when we reached our destination. It was another village, only a little larger than the one we had passed through earlier. There was another concrete building in the center, again with a gas pump and some signs advertising orange pop. Our chauffer filled our car with gas.   On the opposite side of the road from this store and further back was another structure made of concrete blocks. It had no advertising signs outside, only one central door and two windows. A man was seated on an old oil drum by the front door and when he saw my Daddy get out of our car, he quickly rose and hurried over. "Bazia," he said, "welcome to our village. It is an honor that you bring your son to us."

"I appreciate your respect," my Daddy said, " but please, while Toni is here, I wish for him to be treated no differently than any of your other children." At this point,

25

my Daddy turned and waved his hand at me to get out. "Toni," he said, " this is your new home for a while, and this is your new father. You will obey him as if he were me."

The man bowed and nodded, first to my father and then to me, but my Daddy stopped him with a raised palm. "I am serious," he said. "Do not treat him any differently from your other...how many children do you have?"

"Seven," said the man, "Four sons and three daughters."

"Well," said Daddy, handing me my suitcase, "now you have eight. This is your new son, Toni."

Chapter 3: How I Spent My Summer Vacation

As I watched my parents get back in the car and ride off into the dark, I am sure I didn't realize that I would be living here for three months, my entire summer vacation. I could see already that this was going to be very educational if only because my life would be quite different from life in our big family home with all of our servants and guests. I would still have brothers and sisters, in fact, even more than the ones I normally lived with as this man had told my Daddy that he had four boys and three girls, but it was obvious to me from the poverty of this village with its grass huts and an occasional dwelling like this one built of concrete blocks that life here was not as easy as the one I knew. But what I didn't realize was that if I had previously thought the big comfortable home I had left behind sometimes became a crazy place, I had not really understood how emotional and irrational human beings could act. My first meeting with my entire new family was going to be a big shock.

As soon as my parents' car was out of sight, the man who was now my father gestured for me to follow him into the house. He opened the front door and I walked through. Inside, it was pretty dark but I could soon see that there were at least four separate rooms, the biggest one in front across the full width of the building. To my left, there were two wooden straight-backed chairs on a straw mat at one end, like a tiny living room, and to my right was a table and shelves filled with assorted dishes and containers. There was a small icebox in the corner, but during the entire time I lived there, I only saw ice in it once. Mostly the icebox was a cupboard which was tight enough that insects and other food spoilers couldn't get inside. Buying ice to keep food fresh was something of a joke in a climate as hot as Sudan.

The back wall of this long front room had three doors, one open and two closed. Through the open door on the left, I could see a double bed with a pink cotton cover on it and two rather worn-out bed pillows. The floor of this bedroom, like the living room and the kitchen, was dirt. There were no carpets. Behind the first closed door, I could hear a lot of thumping, banging, and an occasional grunt or cry of pain. Then that door opened too and out poured a stream of children. I counted them: there were four boys. The two tallest were wearing T-shirts and shorts, the third only shorts, and the fourth, the smallest boy, nothing at all. As I watched them come into the kitchen, they poked and shoved each other as much as possible so that they looked more like some giant insect with a myriad of different sized arms and legs waving around in confusion.

"Enough," said the father, and he grabbed the tallest boy and slapped him in the face. "Go sit down in the living room," he said as he grabbed the second and repeated the

27

slap, this time a little harder, "You, too, Joseph," he said. He continued to grab and slap all four boys until they were all in the living room, two sitting on the wooden chairs and two on the dirt floor. Then the last door opened and three girls crept out. The father only managed to slap the tallest girl before all of them had dashed into the the kitchen and out of his reach behind the small table. It was then that I noticed there was already a small woman in the corner of the kitchen. She was totally quiet and totally motionless which was why I hadn't seen her at first.

"This is Toni, " said my new father. "He is the son of our chief. He is going to be living with us for a while."

All the children stared at me in silence, but then, the tallest girl in the kitchen spoke. "Why?" she said.

"He was very bad," said the father, "and coming to live with poor hard-working people like us is his punishment."

"What did you do?" asked the girl who was probably about my age.

"I wore the wrong clothes," I answered, and again, there was a stunned silence.

Finally the tallest child, the boy who was sitting in the largest chair in the living room, began to laugh. "How could you wear the wrong clothes?" he said. "How many clothes do you have?"

"A lot," I said, and the laughter stopped and they all stared at me again.
I waited a minute and then spoke again, "But I don't think this is a punishment," I went on, "I think coming to live with you is like a vacation."

28

"A vacation?" The two boys on the living room floor began to laugh hysterically. "We work all day long," they shrieked, falling against each other.

"Doing what?" I said.

"You'll see tomorrow," said the father who was by now I think wanting his chair and a little peace and quiet. "It's time for everyone to go to bed!"

So now all five of us boys went back into the middle room which my new brothers had just tumbled out of. There was no furniture, only a large bundle of grass mats which the second boy immediately began spreading around on the floor.

I looked for another door from this room and found one which I opened. It went outside so I closed it again. and then lifted the curtain over the window. Outside the air was very still. The distant clumps of trees were only black shadows against the grey of fields. There were no other buildings nearby. I had to pee rather badly by now.

"Where is the toilet?" I asked and once again I was greeted by four pairs of astonished eyes and then laughter.

"No toilet, son of our chief," they giggled, and the tallest of the boys took my arm. "I'll show you," he said, and we went out through the back door and then walked about fifty feet from the house toward the clumps of dark trees. The ground was covered with thick vegetation, grasses, and vines, and other unknown plants. I carefully walked behind my new brother, putting my feet in exactly the same spots he did. If there were snakes, I prayed, let him step on them first.

"Careful here," said my new brother, "You see this hole?" There were two tree trunks lying on the ground, forming a sort of V. They hung a little over a rather large hole, a hole which by now I could smell. "That is our toilet, " he said, and proceeded to demonstrate how to pee in it, shooting a stream of urine in an arc up into the air and then letting it splash dramatically in the hole. I jumped back to avoid getting sprayed and he laughed.

"Thank you for showing me," I said as I joined him in relieving my bladder. This was going to be a very interesting vacation.

We were joined almost immediately by the other boys who also peed in the hole and then the youngest proceeded to hang his butt over the side and defecate, but by now I was done, so I walked back to the house with the others. Inside the boys' bedroom was my little suitcase which I opened. The others gathered around and stared as I looked over what my mother had packed. I had several pairs of underpants, one pair of pants, three pairs of shorts, and a half dozen T-shirts. I also had some sox, pajamas, and an extra pair of shoes. "You do have a lot of clothes," said the oldest boy in amazement.

I didn't reply. These were only a few of the clothes I wore and not my best apparel at all. My mother was wise to pack only these older things; she probably knew there would be no need for me to dress up and go to church here. And if any company came, well, I didn't want to look any different from the other children.

The youngest boy, who was still naked, came in through the door to the yard. He grabbed my blue pajamas which were baggy pants and a short-sleeved shirt with buttons, and held them up. "What are these for?" he asked.

"For sleeping in," I answered, and once again, there were shouts of laughter.

"Special clothes for sleeping?" He looked astonished.

"Yes," I said as I took off my shirt and slipped my arms into the blue pajama shirt. They all watched curiously as I buttoned up the top and then took off my pants and underwear and put on the baggy blue trousers. I tightened the waist string. "Which mat is mine?" I asked.

The door from the front room opened and the mother stuck in her head.
She smiled shyly at me. "Toni, did you eat any supper tonight before your parents brought you to us?" she asked.

"No," I said. "I am a little hungry if it would not be too much trouble."

"Come to the kitchen, " she said, but as I tried to follow her, I was almost knocked over by the other boys.

"We're hungry, too, Mama," they said as they jostled and pushed their way through the door.

"You already ate," she said and then ignored their wails of protest. She took a small crock off the shelf and opened it. Inside was a paste of beans and garlic with spices. She spread some of this on a slice of bread she took from the icebox and then rolled it up and handed it to me.

"Thank you, " I said. It was good bean spread, very hot and spicy and I told her so, but I could feel the eyes of my new brothers on me as I got food they obviously wanted so

31

I ate as fast as I could. The mother showed me where there was a big jar full of water on the floor near the table. She gave me a ladle and I dipped out some water for a drink. Again, I thanked her. She watched me shyly the whole time; for a moment, I thought she was going to smile or say something else, but the father suddenly spoke up from the living room.

"Bring the lamp, woman," he yelled, and she quickly took the kerosene lamp from the table and a book of matches and then scurried away.

I went back into the bedroom where my four new brothers were lying on the mats. The three oldest were wearing shorts, but the youngest was still naked. My mat was against the wall next to the front room which made me happy. Now if someone had to go out back in the night, they would not have to step over me. Such a small thing, but I was glad for it. Perhaps, I thought, when you have less, you find more reasons to be grateful for very small blessings, and with that observation, I fell asleep.

I was awakened by the sound of the back door being slammed shut as one of my new brothers went outside to use the bathroom. The other three boys were still sleeping so I quickly opened my suitcase and pulled out some clean shorts and a T-shirt. As I was putting my pajamas into the case, I suddenly realized that there was no big basket for the laundress to take out my dirty clothes. In fact, there was probably no laundress, just that small unsmiling woman who was the wife of my new father and the mother of these seven children. She had been so kind to me the night before, yet my arrival probably meant there would be more work for her to do. I promised myself I would not allow that.

Breakfast was another slice of bread with that good spicy bean paste, and then we all marched out the front door. I followed the whole family around the corner to the right of the house and watched each person take a garden hoe out of a barrel. There was no hoe for me, but the oldest boy shoved his into my hand. "Here, Toni," he said with a big grin, "you can use mine!"

I took it and smiled but just as he let go, his father clouted him across the back of his head. "And you, Sebastian," said the father, "you can take the buckets and refill the water jar in the kitchen! When you finish doing that, bring buckets of water and a dipper out to us in the field. We'll all be needing a drink by then!" Sebastian didn't look so happy now about giving me his hoe, but he didn't argue. He just picked up the buckets and a pole and walked down the road toward the center of the group of grass huts.

I followed the others on a path through a small grove of trees. It was not very hot yet, but birds were already singing loudly and insects buzzing around our heads. As we left the shade of the little jungle, I saw that we were on the edge of a large field. Rows of bean poles were already covered with vines. There were many rows of corn plants too, but it was too early for the ears to form. Around the base of the corn stalks, squash vines twisted and curled from the rows beyond. At the far edge of the field were about a dozen rows of small green plants no more than two feet high. We were headed in that direction., and I followed the other children.

"Now, Toni," said the father, "I don't imagine you have done this before." He pointed to how the others were each standing at the end of a row of the shorter plants and putting the blades of their hoes into the dirt. I shook my head, and he went on, "We have to hoe away all of the weeds that grow up around the plants we need. These are pepper and tomato plants. We'll get a lot of food from them if the weeds don't choke them out, so every day, we have to scrape up the weeds with our hoes. If you see a really big weed, one that somehow got missed during our work from a few days before, then you grab it and pull it out with all its roots." He reached down a few feet up the row in front of us and grabbed a plant which was taller than the others in the row. This plant had very small leaves and some pinkish flowers on it. It looked different from the ones in the row nearby. As he yanked, I could see that the soil around this plant loosened and it came up, dangling a bunch of roots on the end. I nodded that I understood and began to work my way up the row with my hoe. There weren't many big weeds, but I did see a few that were the same size as the plants I was hoeing.

"Be careful," said the father. "Don't put your hoe too close to the plants we want to keep, and don't dig down too deep or you'll cut into their roots and they'll die." Again I nodded.

After that, it was just a matter of working my way up the long row of plants. Each of us children worked one row on our own from one end to the other. The mother also took a row, but the father didn't. He was watching everyone to make sure they didn't skip a spot or miss a weed.

It was slow work and getting hotter all the time, but I guessed that it took about an hour for each of us to finish our own row. There were still four rows of short plants left because there were only eight of us working (Sebastian was still not back with our water), so I went to the next row and began working. The mother began another, and the father told two of the girls to do the last two.

"Joseph," he said, poking the second oldest boy with the handle of his unused hoe, "Go see where your lazy brother is hiding! He should have brought us some drinking water by now!"

"I'm here, I'm here," Sebastian was trotting up the path to the garden with a pole slung over his shoulders. A bucket full of water was dangling from each end of the pole, the water sloshing and dripping.

"Slow down," said the father, "You'll spill it all!" I wondered to myself what he would have said if Sebastian had been walking slowly. Probably tell him to run! This man was very difficult to please.

Sebastian stopped at the edge of the garden and bent over, lowering the buckets to the ground. In one hand, he held a sort of scoop made from a plastic jug. He handed it to his father who dipped it into one bucket and then drank from it. The other children lined up behind the father, and one by one, we all drank several scoops full, the mother drinking last.
I was in front of her in line, and when I was finished, I filled the dipper and turned to hand it to her. She smiled a little as she took it from me, but she didn't speak.

The father had given Sebastian the hoe *he* was supposed to be using and pointed at the other end of the garden where the bean poles were. "You go over there and work with your brothers and Sarah," he said, "and be very careful to get under the bean poles and hand pull all the new weeds. Don't use your hoe in there! Tell the others to be careful!" Then he picked up the dipper and got himself another scoop of water.

By the time the sun was directly overhead, we had finished

hoeing and weeding all the tomatoes, peppers, and beans, and started on the corn rows. The mother disappeared at this point with the youngest girl; they seemed to be headed for the house. The father told us we could take a break to get a drink or go to the hole to pee, but we'd better be quick about it. I took only one break to go back to the house and use the hole; I was sweating so much that I didn't need to.

When I was walking back to the field, I saw the mother carrying a basket of bread. The youngest girl was beside her with the pot of bean paste and a small wide spreader. Lunch would be the same as breakfast, I gathered. Well, the bean paste was good, I thought to myself and the work was making me very hungry.

"Ok, time for food," said the father just as I returned and once again, we lined up, him first, and the rest of us behind him. The mother would pass a slice of flat bread to the littlest girl who then spread it with bean paste. We each took our portion and sat down in the dirt. The sun beat down on our heads as we ate. A few flies came up to examine my lunch, but I waved them away. I watched the other children; they were eating very slowly, and I smiled. This was probably the only way we would get a break until today's job was done, and they wanted to make it last as long as they could. I took a bite and chewed thoughtfully. The air was very hot. And my hands, which had never done anything as difficult as hoeing rows of crops were very sore. My palms were covered with little white pockets of water which were puffy; in a few spots, the water pockets had broken and raw red flesh appeared beneath. Blisters, I thought, remembering one I earned when I helped a gardener rake the lawn one day; that one had healed quickly and I never got another because my Daddy forbid me to ever help the servants again, but now my hands were a very ugly mass of oozing sores. Whenever I wiped my forehead, the salt in my sweat made the blisters hurt even more.

"Ok, boys, " said the father, "hurry up and finish. Get a drink and then let's get this job done." He nodded at his wife, "You and the girls can go back to the house now. It needs a good sweeping out!"

There was a groan of envy from the boys which was quickly stifled when their father glared at them. I could understand their desire to get out of the sun for just a little while.

It took about another two hours to finish hoeing the rows of corn and then we pulled weeds by hand from between the squash plants. The father still did very little to help. He supervised. In fact, at one point, he moved some distance away from the field and sat down in the shade of a large tree. He leaned his back against the trunk, folded his arms, and watched us work. The sun beat down.

When we were all standing at the end of the last row of squash plants, he got up and came back. "Ok," he said, " gather up all those dead weeds and throw them in the bush. We don't want them spreading their seeds in between the rows as they die, now do we?" I nodded and began to gather an armload of weeds. That was something I hadn't thought of.

Disposing of the weeds was only common sense. I didn't know how fast weeds could grow, but I certainly had no desire to pull up or hoe out the children of the ones I had killed today in a week or two. The other boys quickly gathered up their bundles. This activity seemed to mark the end of the gardening for today.

"Okay, Toni," said the father, as I returned from the wilder area where I had thrown the weeds, "let's see how strong you are." He indicated that I should stand in front of him and hold my arms out straight. He put the pole over my shoulders and told me to hold onto it. Then he put a half-empty water bucket on one end. I staggered slightly, but when he put the other bucket on the other side to balance it, I felt better. It was heavy, but years of Daddy's discipline had given me a strong pair of shoulders and arms. Sebastian looked a little surprised. He was at least a half foot taller than me. I am sure he had expected me to fall down.

"Take those back to the house," said the father. I nodded and headed down the path. Sebastian was skipping in front of me, carrying my hoe and his. He seemed pretty happy about the situation, but his father noticed and shouted as we headed into the little patch of trees, "Oh, Sebastian, after Toni dumps those two buckets in the kitchen, show him where the well is in the village. And then, you refill the buckets and carry them back."

Sebastian stopped skipping so quickly I almost ran into him.

Chapter Four: A Learning Experience

As I carried the pole with the two half-empty buckets of water back to the house, my shoulders began to ache. I was reminded for a minute of home, kneeling in a circle with my brothers and sister and holding out our bricks. I wondered if any of them had misbehaved while I was gone and if they too were presently suffering from the fatigue and strain of the punishment, but I also realized that other than my Daddy's punishment, compared to my new family and my new siblings, I really knew very little about physical pain. They had to work in the garden, carry the buckets of water, and probably do other kinds of manual labor on a daily basis which I was completely unaccustomed to. In addition, their father struck them frequently which must have hurt not only their bodies but their spirits. I remembered what my Daddy once said when he saw a neighbor caning his son in the yard in front of their house.

"That is not good discipline," Daddy said. " The pain drives out the lesson of remembering what the boy did wrong. All he can think of when the stick strikes him is that it hurts and it is his father who is hurting him. In addition, his father has put the act of disciplining his son on public display. He is making sure everyone knows he is a good and dutiful father, but he is also telling the world that his child is a bad son. This damages the boy beyond his body and will also create shame and resentment in future years."

By now we had reached the house and Sebastian opened the front door. I lowered both buckets to the ground by bending my knees and then slid the pole off my shoulders. I picked up one bucket and carried it into the house. Sebastian came in, too, and pointed to the kitchen.

"You see that big jar?" he said, pointing to a large ceramic vessel on the floor under the one window in the area. "Pour the water in there." I did as he instructed and carried the empty bucket back outside. I noticed that Sebastian had easily assumed his father's role in our relationship; he could have helped finish the task by bringing in the second bucket when I brought in the first, but he didn't. He stood in the living room, rocking back and forth on his heels and humming while I lugged the second bucket into the kitchen and emptied it.

When I came back outside, he had the pole over his own shoulders. His father had told him to fetch more water, and although he certainly was tired and didn't want to, he didn't dare risk disobedience and the slaps, or possibly a caning, that might follow.
"Put the buckets on the pole, " he said wearily.

"Wait a minute, " I said. "How many trips are we supposed to make?"

Sebastian looked at me. "We have to fill these buckets at least three times. Six buckets of water will get used before tomorrow. So, three trips."

"Is there another bucket?" I asked. Sebastian nodded and pointed to the side of the house where the hoes were stored in a large barrel. I got the other bucket and returned to where Sebastian was standing. "Put the pole down," I said.

Sebastian stared at me. "What, you want to carry the buckets to and from the well?"

I shook my head no, but picked up the pole. I hung the handle of one bucket halfway down the pole. "Turn around," I said as I placed the end of the pole on Sebastian's left shoulder. "Wait a minute," I added and I put the other end of the pole on my right shoulder. Sebastian looked back at me. "Now, when I count to three, bend your knees and pick up the other bucket. One, two three! Put that bucket's handle over the end of the pole in front of you." We were a little clumsy with this maneuver, but we did it. Mine was harder because I had to put the handle over the pole where it stuck out behind me.

40

"Now stand up, " I instructed, and Sebastian and I both rose to our full height. He was a little taller than me but not so much that it would cause a problem when we returned with full buckets.

"Okay," I said, "lead me to the well." Sebastian still seemed a little confused by the change in procedure, but I was sure that by the time we got to the well, he would have figured it out. The two of us working together could fetch the required number of buckets of water with one less trip this way and with less effort because we were really only carrying one and half buckets each. As we walked down the path and into the circle of grass huts that were built around the well, several people who were outside sitting in the shade or cooking over open fires stopped what they were doing to look at us. One old man smiled and nodded, revealing his almost toothless mouth as he muttered to us, "Good boys, good boys, yes, that is a good way to do it!" Sebastian's shoulders rose a little, as if this praise went straight to his heart. He walked with a lighter step as we approached the well.

"This is it, Toni," my new brother said, speaking my name for the first time.

"Tell me when you are ready to bend down," I said, making sure that everyone knew he was in charge.

"On the count of three, " said Sebastian, and he counted. We both dipped down on three and set the buckets and the pole on the ground. Then we filled all three buckets. Sebastian slid the pole through the one that would swing from the middle of the pole, but left the pole on the ground. Both of the other buckets were by his feet, next to the well, and I asked him to wait while I put one of them over the end of the pole near my feet.. Sebastian nodded. He saw the difficulty of putting a full bucket over the end of the pole, especially when the end of the pole was behind you.

"Okay, Toni, " he said, "I think this is the tricky part!" I nodded and then he turned his back to me, bent down, and slipped his end of the pole through the handle of the remaining bucket. "On three, " Sebastian said, and we both dipped down and slid the pole over our shoulders, his on his left shoulder and mine on my right. It was beautifully executed dance, and there was a murmur of appreciation from the people watching.

"I will remember what you told me, brother," I said. "I promise to walk slowly."

"Yes," said Sebastian, "or you will spill all of this nice water and we'll have to do it all again!" He walked around in an arc so that he was in the lead and I pivoted carefully with my end. Only a little water slopped out of the center bucket which had started to swing, but we paused until that stopped and headed back for the house. When we passed the toothless old man, he repeated his praise, "Good boys! Good boys! Very clever!", and although I couldn't see his face, I was pretty sure that Sebastian was smiling. His shoulders were very square and proud.

Back at the house, we emptied the buckets quickly and set off for the well again. The second time we returned, the father was sitting out by the front door. He was frowning. "I never told you to carry the water that way, " he said in a somewhat grumpy manner.
"Whose idea was this?"

"Toni's," said Sebastian, and then he added, "and we only

had to go to the well twice." We did our little dip and drop trick and quickly brought the buckets into the house and dumped them. Sebastian moved very fast and picked up the last one before I had a chance to take it.

"Really?" said the father, and he walked into the house. "I'm just going to check on that water jar, " he added. "If it isn't full, you know what you'll get!"

I watched Sebastian's smile vanish and his shoulders slump. There was silence in the house and then the father returned. "It will do," he said and then without another word, he disappeared around the other side of the house.

Sebastian and I followed him. My sisters were standing next to a circle of rocks surrounding a small fire. The girls were feeding chunks of wood and branches into the flames. My younger brothers were breaking the longest branches into pieces by balancing them on two rocks and then jumping on them. By the house, my new mother was putting pieces of vegetables in a large pot with a tight lid. It was made out of scrap metal riveted together. The top had a piece cut out of it like a vent.

"Can I help you?" I asked the woman and she looked up at me with alarm.

"No," she said, "this work is for women," and she waved her hand to call the oldest of the girls over to her. "Sarah," she said, "get me a large dipper of water from the jug in the kitchen, and one of the chicken bouillion squares. I will also need the blue bowl. Fill it with rice."

"That's a lot to carry," I said to Sarah. "Why don't you hand it out to me through the window?" The little girl smiled, nodded, and then scurried inside. I waited a

43

minute and then one at a time, she handed me the blue bowl, the chicken flavoring, and the dipper of water.

The mother finished putting the cut-up pieces of vegetables in the cooker. It looked like a mixture of onions, sweet potatoes, squash, and carrots. There were also some cabbage leaves which she had torn into strips. She then added the water, the rice, and the chicken flavor square. "No meat today, Toni," she said, "but we will kill a chicken on Sunday."

By now the fire was blazing and I watched as the mother lugged the metal cooker over and balanced it on the rocks over the flames. Her husband and the boys watched also. Didn't they care that the cooker was heavy? Weren't they concerned that she might burn herself? I had never seen anyone prepare a meal this way; in our house, the servants did all of the food preparation in a kitchen which was at the back. They cooked on a gas stove in big pots and frying pans. When I was little, I used to sneak in there and watch them sometimes. It was always a very interesting and lively process, this making of a meal, with sounds of knives chopping, and the head cook giving directions, and the girls chattering and laughing together. But in this family, nothing seemed to be fun at all.

For the rest of that day, I sat under a tree in the shade watching my new brothers and sisters. The girls hung around their mother and occasionally disappeared into the bush to fetch more wood for the fire, but the boys hardly stopped moving. If one of them sat down for a minute, another would sneak up behind him and cuff him in the head or shoulder so that the victim now felt required to leap up and chase his attacker until he caught him and hit him back. The youngest boy at one point had found an interesting long branch which was very flexible. He walked

44

around with it for a while, thrashing small plants and bushes with it until they were ripped to shreds, but then the second oldest boy, Joseph, grabbed it away from him and the chase was on.

Eventually Sebastian came over and sat down next to me. We watched the others in their mad dashing for a while, and then he asked, "Don't you like to play, Toni?"

"I like to play, " I replied, "but not to hurt." I picked up a few small sticks from the ground in front of me and stuck them in the dirt close together in a row. I studied what I had done for a while. "Hand me that skinny branch, please, brother," I said to Sebastian, pointing to a longish twig that was near him but just beyond my reach.
When he gave it to me, I carefully broke it into even lengths, the same size as the pieces I had already stuck in the ground. I made another row of twigs at right angles to the first, forming the second side of a square. Then I studied my creation again. "I need more pieces," I said.

Sebastian's curiosity got the better of him, so for the next fifteen minutes, he scoured the area looking for twigs of a similar thickness to bring back to me. In a short time, I was able to complete two more sides to the square of upright twigs, but the last side had a space in the middle, like a gateway into a fenced area. "Now I need grass," I said, "and it should be long and dry." Sebastian nodded and walked out into the field that bordered the yard where we were all waiting for the evening meal. While he looked for thatch, I laid some of the longer twigs across the top of the uprights. When he returned, I carefully placed the tufts of grass on these supports. Then I began to pick up small pebbles and place them in a double row leading away from the space in the fourth wall.

45

Sebastian suddenly smiled. "It's a house!" he said. "Hey, Joseph, come and look at this! Toni's made a little house!"

Joseph had been straddling his younger brother's chest and laughing at his attempts to free himself, but Sebastian's remarks got his interest. He came over to look at my house, but before he could get there, the youngest boy pushed past him, ran up to us, and kicked the little house apart. Then he ran away into the trees.

Sebastian shot to his feet and started after him, but I put my hand on his leg, "Don't upset yourself, my brother," I said. "It is easily fixed," and I began rebuilding the house immediately. Only one long twig used in building the roof was broken and that was easily replaced.

"That's a nice house, " said Joseph. "I think I'll make one, too." In a short time, there was a whole village of little thatched huts with little pebble paths connecting all of the doorways to a broad road six pebbles wide that ran down the middle. Not all of my brothers and sisters actually constructed the dwellings, but they all watched, even the littlest one who had by now returned from the trees when he realized nobody was paying any attention to him.

I watched him as he walked toward the little house his sister was building, and for a minute, I thought I saw him getting ready to kick it down, but he stopped when he saw that I was watching. "What's your name?" I asked.

"I'm Carlo," he said.

"Nice to meet you, Carlo," I replied. "I think you are the same age as my brother at home. He's five."

"I'm only four, " said Carlo.

46

"Ah," I said, looking at him in amazement, "you are very big for your age. I think you may even be bigger than my little brother!" Carlo stuck out his chest and nodded smugly.

At this point the mother sent the girls into the house to get the bowls and spoons. I could smell the roasted vegetables and my stomach growled. Then she bent over with a thick cloth in each hand so she could lift the hot cooker off the fire. I poked Sebastian. "Let's help her, " I whispered. For a moment, he glanced at his father who was dozing under a tree, but when he saw that the man's eyes were closed, he nodded and we both hurried up to the fire. I motioned to the mother to hand me the thick cloth pads, and I gave two to Sebastian. I held the two I had on either side of the metal container and we quickly shifted it to the ground about two feet away from the fire. It was a very painful task for me because the heat of the pot went right through the pads and made my blisters twitch, but I grit my teeth and refused to drop the cooker. The pain would not last so very long! And the cooker was very heavy for this little tiny woman!

Sebastian and I handed the cloth pads to his mother, and then we each took a bowl and a spoon from the girls and lined up. The mother raised her hand for us to wait.

"My husband," she called. "the food is ready."

At this the father woke up and walked in front of us to the head of the line. She served him a generous amount of rice and vegetables and then dished out the remainder to us.
I was very hungry and ate all of mine rapidly, but when I walked casually next to the cooker and glanced in, I saw

47

that it was empty. Oh, well, I thought, I will not get fat here!

I noticed the mother was watching me walk around. She appeared to be studying me cautiously, glancing quickly at me and then checking to make sure her husband wasn't watching.

Suddenly he jumped up from where he was resting with his back against a tree and announced, "I am going into the village to talk to the men!" He marched off toward the path Sebastian and I had taken to the well, and when he was out of sight, there seemed to be a change in the mood of the mother and the children. It was as if everyone took a small collective sigh and relaxed. I had seen such a reaction before at my home, but it was from the servants whenever my Daddy left for the day, and I thought to myself that for one's wife and children to be relieved to see the man of the house depart, it must mean that something was not right. I wondered if there was a way to change this.

As I sat thinking about what I had seen, the mother approached me shyly. "Let me see your hands, Toni," she asked. I held them out, and she studied the raw blisters on my palms. "These must be taken care of," she said with alarm. "They must be cleaned and we must put some salt on them to kill the badness that the dirt brought in. It will hurt," she added, "but then I will put something on them to make them feel better. I will help you with this until they heal. Your hands will get tougher!"

She took me into the kitchen and filled a large bowl with water from the ceramic vessel on the floor. Then she poured salt into the water. Now she took a clean rag and began to wash the dirt off my hands with the salty water.

It stung a lot, just as my sweat had stung the opened blisters earlier in the day, but after a while, the stinging stopped. When she was satisfied that she had washed away all the dirt, she told me to put both my hands into the salty water. We stood there silently for about ten minutes while my hands soaked in the bowl. Outside, it was growing dark. I could hear the calls of the night birds beginning, and the chirp and click of many insects. My new brothers and sisters were happily adding a few more houses to the village. The sounds of their comments, "This could be the grandfather's house! Here is where we should put the well! What can we use for a gas pump?", made me smile.

The mother took a larger clean rag from the shelf behind her, "Let me dry your hands now, Toni," she said, "and I will put something on them to keep the skin from getting too tight as it heals." She took a large crock down from the shelf and removed the lid. Inside was lard, the hardened fat from animals. She put a large glob of it on my dry hands and told me to rub all over my palms. "We will do this every day," she said, "until they heal and get strong." She paused and then continued, "I don't think my husband will object; after all, he wouldn't want to report to our chief that his son got sick while in his care!"

Chapter Five: Picking Mangos

The days of my summer vacation sped by as I worked in the hot sun with my brothers and sisters. I learned that the boy whose name I didn't know, the second to the youngest, was Peter. He was the quietest child and the most curious. I came into the boys' bedroom once and found him examining the contents of my suitcase. When he looked up and saw me watching him, he slammed it shut so quickly he pinched his fingers. For the rest of the day, he watched me. I think he was waiting for me to tell his father what I had caught him doing, but I never said a word.

The girls were named Sarah, Suzette, and Rebecca, oldest to youngest. I didn't get to know them as well as the boys because they were all as shy as their mother and stuck close to her.

I did see a friendly girl in the village named Mary who often came out of her house when Sebastian and I walked through with the buckets on our way to the well. She always smiled at me. I decided she liked me, so I smiled back. She looked to be about my age, but since there was never any time to mingle with the people in the village, our friendship didn't get any further than smiles and glances. Sebastian caught us looking at each other once; he seemed to find it amusing and would wiggle his eyebrows up and down as if this was a very ardent romance.

For a brief time in the middle of the rainy season, we had to walk about twice as far to the other side of the village to fill our buckets because the big well was almost dry. This other water source was not a true well with a wall around the water and a cover on the top, but a pipe that stuck out of the ground with a pump attached. Sebastian and I would take turns pumping while the other one held the bucket. The water from this source was very cold, and although the pipe was further away, I liked to go there because this water made a very refreshing drink on a hot day. It also had a slightly metallic taste.

Once a week we would get up before the sun rose, put our dirty clothes in baskets, and walk to the other end of the village where there was a river of swiftly running water. It was there that I learned to wash my own clothes, using a small piece of soap to scrub, then rubbing the fabric and rinsing until they were clean. We would carry the wet clothes back to the house in the baskets and spread them over bushes to dry in the sun. On laundry day, we ate our breakfast while walking to whatever field or grove we would work in that day because the father was always in a hurry for us to get to work.

There were three different gardens to hoe and weed, all in different directions from the house. There were also mangos to pick from the huge grove which belonged to the father of this family. Two kinds of mangoes grow in Sudan; I never learned their names, but one is longer and bigger while the other kind is smaller. Both kinds grew in the family's grove, but the larger ones were the cash crop. They were slightly sweeter which made them a very attractive product to sell in distant villages or even the city. We picked these green and called them "long distance mangoes" because they would ripen as they were carried by a man with a bicycle to the distant market. The smaller mangoes were picked when they were ripe and sold locally to the villagers or eaten occasionally by us!

Picking involved being assigned to a team of pickers or packers. The pickers (and I was usually given this job along with Sebastian, Joseph, and Sarah) carried long poles with sharp curved blades on the ends. It was the job of each picker to find a ripening mango and sever its stem from the tree so that it fell with a thump on the ground. If I had thought my arms ached after holding up bricks or hoeing, it was nothing to the pain of marching around a grove of trees holding a heavy pole erect over my head. The father occasionally gave us short breaks, but we would work at picking mangos, either long distance or local, until the sun was directly overhead. By then we had usually picked plenty for the bicycle man to take to market.

51

The packers, the younger children, would pile the fruit in baskets around the grove. At first I was surprised to see that falling all that way to the ground didn't bruise the fruit, but after a while as I labored in the hot sun, even I fell victim to the mindlessness of the work and didn't bother my brain with wondering about anything except how soon we would finish for the day.

The last task in the mango grove was always gathering all of the baskets and bringing them down by the house. By the time we were finished, the man who would bring them to the market was usually there. I was always surprised to see how skillfully he balanced the loads of mangos in baskets which were attached to the sides of his bicycle. Then he would climb on and ride away with barely a shift to the right or the left.

At some point after I arrived in the village, about the time that the main well went dry, it was decided that the water in the river was being wasted as it rushed away to the south. "We need to dig a pond," said my father, "and we need to place it here." He pointed to a large flat open area about half-way between his house and the rest of the village.

"That will be very convenient for you," muttered the toothless old man who often smiled and said hello to me when I walked by on my way to the pump with Sebastian.

"And for you, grandfather," said my temporary father. "I will have my children dig this pond. There won't be as much for them to do as the weather gets dryer."

My brothers and sisters and I all looked at each other. I said nothing, but they all heaved great sighs and rolled

52

their eyes.

Thus it was that after a morning of picking mangos, we worked our arms and shoulders in the opposite direction by heaving thick clods of heavy clay soil into piles around the perimeter of what would become the village pond. When we started digging at the top where the river ran into the field, we dug in a gentle arc perpendicular to the stream, but when we began to work our way down the sides, I noticed that a little bulge was developing on the left side. It reminded me of something.

The following morning I got up earlier than the others and went into the woods to cut some large branches. When I got back to the house, my temporary mother looked out the window. "Toni, why are you up so early?" she said. "Laundry day isn't until tomorrow!"

"I know," I said. "This is for something else. I have an idea."

I carried the poles, about fifteen of them, to the area where we were digging the pond. Then I stuck them one at a time in different spots. From time to time, I would walk down to the bottom of the field near our house and look at them. They seemed to lining up just the way I wanted them. My plan was going to work.

That morning, as I expected, we picked long-distance mangos until lunch. After we ate, we headed toward the field.

"What are the poles for?" said Sebastian. He knew by now that any unusual event was probably something I had come up with.

"They are marking the borders of the pond," I said.

"But it's not round!" said Carlo.

"It's better than round," I said. "It is a very special shape. It is the shape of Africa!"
I went on to explain to them that the pond we were digging was big enough that it would be seen if a plane flew overhead, and that I was sure that anyone who looked down from the plane would be amazed to see a pond in the shape of our great continent of Africa in the middle of the bush.

"Wow," said Carlo. He walked around the poles carefully. "It doesn't look like much yet," he said.

"Then we better get digging," I said.

We finished digging the pond two weeks into August, about seventy days from the day my mother and father had left me here in this village. At first I had thought of my parents, my brothers and sister, the servants, and the other friends and relations I left at home often, but after a while I focused more on the changes I could see happening in my new family. I thought sometimes to myself that if my Daddy could see me, he would see that here in this little village as a member of this family, I was learning to be a chief.

My influence was subtle, but steady. I didn't tell any of them what to do, but in a short time, there was less fighting and hitting and more cooperation. Whenever I could, I set the example, but after a while, that was no longer necessary. Sebastian copied me, and slowly, the others copied him.

54

And then came the day when the pond was finished, weeks ahead of schedule. Everyone in the village walked around it, remarking on the unusual shape. All of my brothers and sisters stood silently by, beaming at the smiles on their neighbors' faces, but when the toothless old man stopped at the foot of the pond where the stream ran out of South Africa, Carlo couldn't contain himself any longer.

"It's Africa," he shouted. "Can you see it?"

Everyone stopped walking for a minute, and then the grandfather spoke up, "Yes, it is! I can see it!" He pointed up to the right where we were standing. "There is the Horn of Africa, Somalia, Ethiopia, and our country, Sudan!"

Suddenly everyone in the crowd who knew anything about geography was pointing to where a country or city would be. There was great excitement as everyone in the village walked around the pond and examined it from different sides. As families walked along the coastline, some pointed to places they themselves had traveled. I heard one woman speaking to her son who looked to be about my age, "Samuel, do you remember your grandmother? Your father's mother? She came from Zimbabwe which would be right," she pointed further into the pond, "there!"

The toothless old man spoke up again, "I think the school teacher will be very surprised to see this when he returns!"

"And when will that be, grandfather?" I asked.

"In about two weeks," he replied.

My foster father spoke up at this point, "You will not be here then, Toni. You will go back to your family when school starts. Your father made that very clear."

55

My heart leaped in my throat, but I remained calm. Two weeks was still long enough away that I could not afford to start thinking of it. I must focus on today and tomorrow and maybe the day after that, but too much dreaming of a time yet to come would take away my strength and release powerful emotions. So far I had kept my dignity as a chief's son should. I would not let myself act like a little child now.

Sebastian was watching me, "Are you eager to go home, my brother?" He had taken to calling me that lately and I took it as a sign that he liked me and had accepted me as a part of his life.

"A little," I answered, not wanting to be dishonest. "But I will miss all of you, my special family, and I will miss this village and the people in it." On the other side of the pond, Mary was once again smiling at me. Perhaps I could get to talk with her before I left. She did seem like a sweet friendly girl.

"Toni," my foster father said, "I would like to talk with you alone. Please come back to the house with me."

I nodded and followed him as the others continued to walk around the pond and talk about what an amazing accomplishment it was. I noticed that Carlo was especially proud of it; he had worked very hard, shoveling and digging beside me in the hot sun for many days. And now he was getting the attention and praise he richly deserved. All of my brothers and sisters deserved credit for this pond. I had dug alongside of them, and yes, using the shape of Africa had been my idea, but without them, I would still be digging. There was no way I could have completed this dream on my own in such a short time. Many years later, I would remember digging this pond and I would realize that it was an important lesson in how to lead people and help them work together, but at the time, I had no idea how important this experience would prove to be. I was still a child, and, although I already had a sense of my own purpose in this world, I didn't realize that God was giving me lessons that would help me fulfill His plan.

When we got to the house, we went inside. My father sat down and then indicated that I should sit opposite him in the other living room chair. "I wanted to tell you something, " he said, "about what your mother and father expected from you when they left you here."

I nodded, and he went on. "They thought you would run away." I was a little surprised; except for my thought in the car that it would be a long walk home, I hadn't considered running away at all. Now I was puzzled, too. Apparently my family didn't know me as well as I thought; they seemed to think I was cowardly and couldn't face a challenge. At least, for me, that was what it would have meant if I had run away.

"But you didn't," said my foster father, " and I was surprised at this too. I know that any one of my children would have run away if I had sent them to live with a family whose living conditions were worse than ours." He chuckled, " And the differences between your home, the home of our chief, and this home are probably beyond my imaginings." He stuffed some tobacco in his little pipe and lit it as he considered me some more. "What was the biggest difference, Toni?" he asked.

I thought for a moment; there were indeed many differences, less food and food of lower quality, sleeping on the floor, no showers, no clean clothes (unless I washed

57

them myself), and a great deal of physical labor, far more than I had ever done. I had recently noticed that the muscles in my arms especially were much harder and larger. I also didn't get tired now as much as I had at first, although each night I slept the dreamless sleep of exhaustion on the floor mats. But the biggest difference? I smiled before I answered him.

"The biggest difference was how you discipline your children, " I said.

My foster father frowned, "Because I slap them, and sometimes I cane them? Doesn't your father do that? Or does a servant take care of the actual punishment? I can't imagine all of you being perfectly behaved little ladies and gentlemen all the time. In fact, watching you and seeing how polite and quiet you are, I was certain that the rod had been applied a lot on you from an early age."

I stared at him. "I have never been beaten or hit," I said calmly. And then I told him about the kneeling and the bricks. "That is the only punishment my Daddy ever uses," I explained. "He says that striking a child makes him nervous and jumpy. He says that the child will remember the caning but often he will forget why it was given. The pain and the humiliation drive every thought out of his head."

The father said, "I never thought of that. I am sure your father has good reason to think this. Was it something he learned in the army?"

"I'm not sure," I answered, "but I do know that whenever one of us does something bad, he punishes us all. That is from the military. Also, he spends a lot of time explaining to us what we did wrong, why we are being punished, and that he does not do this to hurt us, but to teach us."

The father nodded again. "That sounds like our chief, Henry Bazia," he said. "Before you came to us, he visited me and explained that this was an experiment, that you were proving to be, in some ways, a difficult child, but before he made a judgment about you, he wanted to find out what kind of person you are." He puffed a few times on the pipe. "If you had run away, I am sure he would have thought very differently about you from what he will after I report what I have seen in you." He looked out the window and smoked some more.

Then he went on, "You have changed my family. You have made them work harder and better together. The big ones don't bully and hurt the small ones the way they used to. And when they work, they work with more thought and care."

I nodded, "If you don't mind me speaking?" I raised my eyebrows and looked at him with great respect. He might not be the perfect father, but he was my elder and I was still living under his roof. It would not do to insult him.

"No, please speak what you think," my foster father said.

"They will cooperate more and work even harder if you follow my Daddy's example and stop hitting them, and if once in a while you tell them they have done well. It doesn't have to be often, but your sons especially look to you for approval and praise. Your good words always mean a lot to them."

"I see the wisdom of this, " said my foster father. He took a puff from his pipe and blew a smoke ring across the room. When I laughed at this, he smiled at me and then said, "Toni, I think you will be a great chief someday."

I thanked him for the compliment; after all, I had just told him that praise from time to time was good for children. But I didn't tell him that I was unlikely to be the next chief of our tribe. After all, I was the second son. My older brother Bazia would be the next chief, following our tribal tradition.

Chapter Six: Sebastian's Dream

The next two weeks were very busy because many of the vegetables in the garden were ready to pick and sell. The man with bicycle came every other day, and we loaded him up with squash, corn, tomatoes, peppers, and, of course, more mangos. Now that the pond in front of our house was done, we would wash our clothes at the end of our workday rather than getting up early on a special day to walk to the river. This, of course, gave us more time to work on the harvesting. My foster father was an ambitious man. He didn't want to waste any of the resources left to him in the land by his father. I only wished I had been able to teach him to work alongside his family rather than standing off at a distance and managing the labor. But it wasn't my place to speak about his behavior to him.

I did get to talk with the sweet girl Mary in the village a couple of times. She was very shy, so I didn't learn much about her. Her mother, on the other hand, was very eager for me to get to know her daughter. I could tell because if I came into the village alone, perhaps to get two buckets of water or deliver a basket of small mangos, as I was walking by Mary's hut, I could hear her mother inside telling her to get outside and smile at "the little chief". Hearing this made me sad; now I didn't know whether Mary liked me for myself or because her mother wanted her to get to know

60

the son of their tribal chief. I continued to be friendly to Mary however; it wasn't her fault that her mother was pushy. This hadn't happened to me before, but I had seen it happen many times with my older brother, and as I grew older, it became more and more of a problem for me. In Africa, leaders are considered as royalty, and any connection to them is an advantage over other people. I would often not know whether someone tried to befriend because he or she liked me, a chocolate boy, or because they wanted to gain status from my family name, Bazia.

The schoolmaster returned to the village a week before school would resume and was welcomed with a special feast; everyone who had children brought special food to the gathering which was held right beside the new pond. He also had a hut of his very own which had been rethatched and cleaned very well. I knew that my father paid his salary, but the villagers were expected to feed and house him. I wondered if he would comment about the shape of the pond, but although I could see he recognized what it was, he never said a word. It was as if he didn't accept that a child could have thought of something like this, even the child of a chief. Or perhaps the villagers were so in awe of an educated man that no one had spoken to him about it. I did notice that they treated him with great respect while he seemed to look down on them a little.

When school started, the children in the village were supposed to attend class from eight in the morning until two in the afternoon. There was no school house, just a large open area under a thatched roof off to the west of the village. It also contained a free-standing blackboard, but no chairs or desks. The children had no paper, pencils, or books. They learned their numbers and letters by scratching them in the dirt as they sat or knelt in rows, the youngest in the front going back to children as old as my brother Sebastian who was twelve.

"I may not go to school every day this year," Sebastian said a little sadly. " My father says it is time I worked year round."

"Can you read?" I asked.

"Yes. a little," said my brother, "but..." he paused and then he sighed. "I don't want to be a farmer like my father."

"What do you want to do?" I asked.

"I think I would like to have a store, maybe in the city," he said. "One time, my father went into the city in the back of someone's truck, and I went, too. We delivered a very large picking of long-distance mangos to a shopkeeper who argued with my father for over an hour about the price. While they were dealing, I walked around the store. It was full of amazing things. All kinds of people came in and out all the time to buy. I found it very exciting."

"Do you know your numbers? Can you add and subtract?"

"Yes," said Sebastian, "but there is no way my father will let me leave this village and go to Khartoum. He will make me stay here and work until he dies. Then I will be trapped on the land. And it takes money to start a business."

I thought for a moment and then I said, "Sebastian, try to go to school as much as possible, even if it means making a deal with your father by promising to work very hard after school ends each day. Or maybe you can get up early and work for an hour or two before school. Don't talk to him about your dream, but don't give up on it either. I will talk to my father. He may be able to help you. But remember," I put my finger to my lips, "this is our secret. Say nothing."

Sebastian's eyes were huge with astonishment. "Thank you, my brother," he said. "You have given me hope." There was new happiness in his face on that day, and for many days afterward. His reaction to my words showed me the importance of hope, and I was eager to get back to my home and talk to my father and my Grandpop about this lesson. People cannot be happy without hope. This was one of the many lessons I would take home with me in a few days.

On the Friday before school started, I was very restless. We children had spent the morning picking long-distance mangos, and the bicycle man had already carried them away. My foster father seemed to have no further work for us that day which surprised me.

I knew I was going home before Monday which was the first day of school, but for some reason, I expected my parents to come to get me on Sunday, so I walked around various places on the farm thinking about all of the experiences I had there. I walked through all three gardens, noticing that the area where I had worked at hoeing and weeding when I first arrived was nothing but bare earth. Even the stubble of corn stalks had been turned under. The earth was resting before my foster father planted it again with a late rainy season crop like greens or millet. The second and third gardens still contained vegetables that would be harvested and eaten by the family for some time, although most of the corn was already picked. It, too, was an important cash crop. I walked through the mango grove and found several small mangos which had fallen off the trees by themselves. Two of them weren't too ripe to pick up and save, so I decided to carry them back to the house. Perhaps my foster father would allow me to give them to my parents when they came for me. My mother especially liked mangos.

I was almost at the house when I saw two people walking toward me. It was a man in a suit and a woman wearing a pink dress and holding a flowered parasol over her head. It was my mother and father. For a brief minute, I hadn't recognized them. It was as if my mind had cast a haze over my memory of them; perhaps this was a way to prevent too much longing and unhappiness. But the haze cleared and I realized I was going home two days earlier than I expected.

"Are you ready to go, Toni?" my mother said. "Have you packed your suitcase?"

"Not yet, " I replied and then I handed her the two mangos. "I'll go and pack right away."

"Wait a minute," said my Daddy. He looked me over carefully. "You are bigger!" For several moments, he studied my upper arms which were bare because for months, I had taken to wearing only shorts and rubber tire sandals most of the time. "And you are definitely stronger!" He pointed to my biceps. "Look at the muscles," he said to my mother.

"Were they good to you?" my mother asked.

"As good as they know how to be," I said with a shrug. "I learned a lot."

"And so did they," said my Daddy. "They have been talking about you since we got here." He studied me some more. "Get your things. You're going home."

So I walked quickly toward the house, but when I knew my parents could no longer see me because of twist in the path, I ran. I entered the boys' room through the back and hastily threw all of my clothes, clean and dirty into my suitcase. I also put on a T-shirt, socks, and my regular shoes.

The best outfit I had with me, the one I had been wearing the day my parents dropped me off, no longer fit because I had, indeed, grown taller and broader. Peter, the next to youngest child, was now the same size as I had been at the beginning of the summer vacation, so I folded those clothes and placed them in the corner of the room where he normally spread his sleeping mat.

I smiled to myself as I wondered what he would think when he found them, especially since he had been the one who had looked through my suitcase some time ago. Nothing of mine had been missing, but Peter's reaction to my arrival at that time was full of guilt and fear, so I was pretty sure he had been up to no good.

My Grandpop had frequently told me that it was a wise practice to offer kindness and friendship to all people, but especially to those who might not have offered this goodness to you. "People who lie or cheat you, people who steal from others, these people are not evil, Toni. They are needy. They lie to protect their reputation or to prevent punishment. They cheat or steal because they don't know any other way to get the things they feel they must have or that they see others enjoying. They believe life has treated them unfairly, but if they are given what

65

they need with respect and taught how to get what they need and want for themselves in an honest way, they will cease to lie, cheat, or steal. No person is born evil."

I shut my suitcase and walked out of the room. No one was in the kitchen or the living room, but I could hear my Daddy talking to my foster father in the front yard so I headed that way.

"And you say it was Toni's idea to dig the pond in this shape?" said my Daddy. He was laughing a little, and shaking his head in amazement. "That was pretty clever!"

At this point I heard the pounding of feet and looked toward the village. The schoolmaster was running towards us down the path as fast as he could. When he got within a few feet of my Daddy, he stopped so abruptly he almost fell forward. Sweat was pouring down his brow and he quickly pulled a handkerchief from his pocket and wiped his face. Then he wiped his hands as well and stepped up to my Daddy, holding out his right.

"Sir, sir," he offered his hand to my father to shake, "I didn't know you were here! When someone told me, I came as fast as I could."

"I appreciate your speedy arrival," my Daddy said with a slight smile, "but your haste was not necessary. I did not come to this village to speak with you or examine your work; I came to bring my son home."

The perplexed schoolmaster looked at all of us children. I knew what he was thinking: not one of us was dressed like the child of a tribal chief. Then he spotted the suitcase in my hand, and his mouth fell open. I was certain now that the reason he had said nothing to me or anyone else for that matter about the unusual pond was that he had so distanced himself from the people whose children he taught that they didn't talk to him about the events that occurred while he was away in the city for the summer. In fact, it was unlikely they talked to him at all or that he would have wanted them to. It was a strange thing to me that he didn't know or understand the people he taught and that he didn't appear to even want to. How could you affect the mind of a child unless you also knew what was in his heart?

At this point, my mother gestured toward the car, "Henry," she said very politely, "I believe we need to leave soon."

"Yes," said my Daddy. He shook the schoolmaster's hand, and then the hand of my foster father.

While he did this, I walked up to each of my foster brothers and sisters and did the same thing. When I came to Peter, I leaned forward and whispered, "There is something in our bedroom for you." I saved my handshake for Sebastian for last and whispered a special message to him as well. "Remember our secret," I said and once again I saw the happiness of hope in his eyes. I would have to speak to my Daddy about this as soon as possible, if only to make it easier for Sebastian to continue going to school. He would need a good education if he was going to successfully reach his goal.

I tried to shake hands with my foster mother, but she backed away from me and kept her head down. I had never seen my foster husband strike or abuse her, but I had observed that he wasn't particularly thoughtful or kind. Unfortunately I had not had time to affect all of the changes in this family which I had hoped for, but perhaps eventually the improved attitudes of the children would make her life a little easier. Certainly her daughters loved her. Maybe that was enough.

Then I shook hands respectfully with my foster father and carried my suitcase to the car. I didn't shake hands with the schoolmaster as we had not really met, and he had moved as far away from us as possible after he shook hands with my Daddy. Both my parents followed me to the car and got in. As we drove away, I could hear Carlo yelling, "Goodbye, Toni! Don't forget us!" I knew that I never would.

So once more we drove along the dusty road, back the way I had come three months ago. Once more, we waited and choked on the dust as herds of cattle were driven across the unpaved way before us. My father wiped his brow with his handkerchief and my mother fanned her face with her hand. I looked out at the landscape, now more yellow and brown than the lush green it had been at the beginning of June. In November, the dry season would return, lasting until March. In April, the rains that made our beloved land so fertile returned, and the cycle would begin all over again.

"Toni?" My Daddy spoke so unexpectedly that I jumped a little. "Do you understand why we sent you away?"

"Not exactly," I said. "My foster father only told me what you expected, that I would run away. But I don't really know why I was sent away in the first place."

My Daddy turned in his seat so that I could see his eyes, "We wanted to find out what kind of a person you are."

"Yes," said my mother, interrupting him, which was very unusual, "we wanted to find out if you were an original thinker or if you were just a troublemaker. When you

68

played that little trick with the Sunday clothes, we couldn't tell. And we had both been wondering for some time why you were so different from the rest of our children."

"I know," I said. "You were always saying that I was not your child."

My mother looked uncomfortable and then looked at my Daddy. When he nodded, she went on, "You are my child, Toni. I am certain of that now. I just didn't know how much!"

"Your mother has always been a very original thinker," my Daddy smiled at her, "but much of her story is hers to tell you when she is ready. I have reminded her many times that an original thinker doesn't do what anyone, even his own parents, expect of him. That's the meaning of original." For a moment, my parents both smiled at me and then at each other.

"So," my Daddy went on with his explanation of my unusual summer vacation, "we wanted to see what kind of person you were; this experiment was definitely a success because now we know a lot more about you."

I nodded at him, encouraging him to go on.

"Your foster father said you never complained and that you worked very hard. He was surprised at that because he was as convinced as I was that you might try to run away or at least avoid living like his children. He also said that you set an excellent example for his children by being polite and helpful to everyone. Finally he confessed that he truly didn't understand how you did it, but it seemed to him that his children fought less and cooperated more. The villagers always spoke well of you, too. One old man told us about the new way to carry water buckets. He said that you had tried to create the impression that this wasn't only your idea, that you gave some credit to the oldest boy, but it was obvious to him that it came from you."

I nodded again.

"That showed good leadership. I think you did well."

"Thank you, Daddy," I said. Such words from him were high praise indeed. For a moment, I thought of bringing up the way my foster father had disciplined his children by hitting them as well as the need for my brother and friend, Sebastian, to stay in school so he could fulfill his dream, but there would be time for me to talk to Daddy about this alone. Right now, as I looked down the road, I saw a few familiar houses and I knew that we were almost home. I leaned forward eagerly, as if that could bring me closer to the life of comfort and privilege I had formerly known under my Daddy's umbrella. I must confess that I had missed it, although I hadn't complained once.

"I will have to take you shopping for new clothes," my mother said. "Even shoes, I think. Those look like they are tight!"

"Yes, they are too small now," I said. "That would be good." The driver swung the wheel and we turned onto the drive that led up to our house. The two gardeners were pretending to trim the grass that bordered it, but I knew they were watching for me.

When we pulled alongside, they peeked in the window and smiled, and I waved at them. "He's home!" I heard one say to the other. Yes, I thought to myself, Chocolate Boy is home.

70

Chapter Seven: Home Again

When I got out of the car in front of our house, I felt like I had stepped into some kind of time machine because my two brothers and my sister were standing by the drive just as they had been on the day I rode away three months before. They were also smiling, but it wasn't the same kind of smug boy-are-you-in-for-it smile which had been there in June. It was more like a boy-are-we-glad-to-see-you smile, and then, one by one, they stepped closer to me. My older brother took my suitcase with his left hand and then shook my hand with his right. My sister began jumping up and down and repeating, "You're back, Toni! You're back!" over and over again. My younger brother just looked at me shyly, and then mumbled something about lions.

"What did you say?" I said.

"I said, " he repeated, "I knew the lions couldn't get you !"

"What lions?" I asked.

"Bazia said you would run away into the bush and the lions would get you and eat you!" Batista shook his head in a very determined way, "I told him that there was no way a lion could get you! You're too smart for any dumb old lions."

I looked at my older brother Bazia, who had by now stopped shaking my hand. "Why did you think I would run away?" I asked.

" Because I would have!" said Bazia. "I would have waited until dark on the very first night I was there, I would have crept out of the house when everyone was asleep, and

71

then I would have walked back along the road as fast as I could."

"It would have been a long walk," I pointed out.

"Yes," he went on, " but there is no way I would have stayed in the house of some poor villagers for three whole months. I am Bazia; I am the son of a chief!" He stuck out his chest proudly.

"You would have had to walk for at least a week to get back here," I said. "What would you eat? What would you drink? Where would you sleep when you got tired?"

"I would have stopped at every house or village along the way and told them who I was," my brother said. "They would have been happy to feed me and give me water or juice. They would let me sleep in their houses! Why, they probably would have driven me back in a car if I asked them!"

"If they had a car!" I said.

My brother looked puzzled; he couldn't begin to imagine the lives of the people with whom I had been living for the whole summer, but then, he didn't have to. Such a test of his character wasn't necessary; he was not an original person like me, even though he had grown up under my Daddy's umbrella. My younger sister Ireni and my little brother Batista were rapidly turning out to be the same as him, uniform people, who were more concerned that they fit in with the people around them than being themselves. In fact, I thought to myself, three months with my foster family in the village would have made Bazia or Batista into the kind of unhappy quarrelsome boys that I had seen during my first few weeks there. Ireni, who was a bit headstrong, might have resisted adapting a little longer; after all, she wasn't used to being a quiet timid girl child, but by the end of the second month, she would have been cowering next to my foster mother with the rest of the girls. Three months living there would not have been good for my siblings at all! But it had been very good for me. I had learned so much, not the least of which was that I could still be me without being under the protection of my Daddy's umbrella! Knowing this made me proud.

Bazia headed toward the house, swinging my little suitcase by his side. He continued to describe to Batista the many clever ways he would have survived on his long march back to our house from the village, but I knew he was just making up impressive stories.

"And if you saw a lion?" Batista asked in a trembling voice.

"I would always carry a thick stick, about this long," Bazia spread his arms out as wide as he could, "and if a lion came, I would hit him on the nose!"

"Whaa," cried Batista, "but the lion wouldn't like that! He might come after you!"

"I would hit him again and then I would climb a tree. And I wouldn't come down again until the lion went away."

By now we were at the front door which suddenly swung open. There in the living room were our two most important servants, the back-up men. We called them that because my Daddy insisted that there was no reason why a well-run household should ever be out of anything that was needed. From needles to napkins, hankies to hair ribbons, soap to spices, it didn't matter what it was: if the cry arose in our house that something was not available, one or both

73

of these servants would be looking for a new job. They were our personal shoppers! In fact, they were so important that they even had their own vehicle to drive to and from the market as many times each day as necessary. And with five people in the family as well as the demands of a kitchen with three kitchen servants, a washroom with two laundresses, and a garage with five cars and two drivers, they had plenty of needs to supply. I could recall days when the car they used went back and forth to the market as many as ten times. They were always checking out supply closets or talking to the kitchen staff or the laundresses. Working for my Daddy was one of the best positions around and they didn't want to get fired.

So in letting us all into the house, they were slightly deviating from their normal duties, but after greeting me and welcoming me home, they said they would be in to see me later as they were sure I would be needing some new toiletries. They had stocked the little shelf which was mine in the bathroom with soaps, lotions, powders, and toothpaste, but if there was anything else I needed, they would be by later to write down my requests. They both knew how I loved to take showers and change my clothes several times a day.

My brother started to carry my suitcase into the bedroom where I usually slept, but he was stopped by one of the laundresses. "No, no, young Mr. Bazia, " Rosanne said, "please let me have Mr. Toni's suitcase. I am sure he won't want to unpack it himself and all of the clothes in it probably need washing and ironing, if they haven't already turned into rags!" She picked up the suitcase and scurried down the hall. My brother shrugged and gestured toward my door.

"Welcome home, " he said, and then he went toward his

74

own room.

I walked into my room, Batista close behind me, while Ireni lingered in the doorway.
"Welcome home from me, too," she said. "We missed you." Her expression of confusion at her own admission made me raise my eyebrows in curiosity.

"Why?" I asked. "You are all usually complaining that I cause a lot of trouble, that I am different."

"Yes," said Ireni, "you are different, and you do cause trouble, but...." She thought a moment. "You make things fun," she finally said. Then she, too, headed away, down the hall.

"Why didn't you run away?" said Batista who was sitting in the middle of my bed. "Were you afraid of the lions?" When I didn't answer, he revealed something that only the two of us knew, "Or was it the snakes?" He, too, was afraid of snakes, which is how he came to know my fear. It was our secret, I had told him, and it was very important that he keep this secret. That way, whenever there was a situation where there might be snakes around, like if we went to a park or walked near thick bushes or deep grass, he and I could look at each other and share our fear. If we stood together, I told him, we were stronger than any snake and stronger than our fear.

I had already taught him the trick I used of walking closely behind someone else, letting that person drive the snakes away first. Batista and I didn't share many feelings or experiences, but I had convinced him that sharing a fear made it half as big, and although I wasn't sure that this was really true, it did feel like that sometimes. When I found him shaking and crying behind the house one day

75

because a gardener had startled a snake which ran right in front of him, I had shared this secret with him as a kindness; for several months after that, I had fully expected him to blurt out, "Toni's afraid of snakes, too, just like me," but he never did.

But now it was time to answer his question about running away, so I sat down next to him on the bed. "I didn't run away because it would have been a foolish thing to do," I began. "Running away, unless it's from some real danger, like a lion or a wild dog, doesn't ever do any good. It's better to face a tough situation and learn how to handle it than to run away."
Batista looked at me, his eyes very wide.

I went on, "If you run away from a challenge, you weaken yourself, and the next time you meet a challenge, the first thing you want to do is run away again. After a while, it becomes easier to run away than to face the trouble. I do not want to become like that."

Batista shook his head and looked very sad. I waited. In order to avoid looking at me, he kept his head down and sighed. I waited some more. Finally he said, "I ran away from two boys last month. They were calling me sissy pants. Then, last week, I saw them again, and they called me little baby chief and they walked behind me, singing over and over, little baby chief, little baby chief, so I ran up our driveway as fast as I could. Now I don't walk on the street at all," Batista mumbled. "In fact, I don't even go near the street." He sighed again. "I don't know what to do."

I looked at him; his face was crumpled like he was going to cry and his shoulders were slumped. "Did they come after you or try to hit you? Did they throw rocks?" I had to make

76

sure that my brother wasn't really in danger of getting hurt.

"No," said Batista, "they just called me names."

"Well," I said, "first of all, you know that if they did try to hurt you, you should tell Daddy. Nobody would ever dare hurt the son of the chief!'

"But they did hurt me," said my brother. "They called me names."

"Where did the names strike you?" I asked.

"What?" Batista stared at me now.

"Where did they strike you? Where were you hurt?"

"The words didn't strike me," Batista protested, "but they did hurt. They hurt me." and he pointed to his chest, "Here."

"That's because you took the words personally."

When my brother looked puzzled, I said, "Let me make it simple for you. I know our Daddy says that we are special because we are his children, but let me tell you another secret. We will only be special as long as we live under Daddy's umbrella or as long as he can protect us. Someday, when we each grow up, we will leave this safe home and go out into the world where we are the same as all the other people in the world. In that big world, we are all the same. Nobody is higher and nobody is lower; we are all the same, and God is over all of us."

"Only God." I emphasized my point by moving my first

finger in an arc over both of us. "So when someone says something to you to make you lower than him, you must smile at him and say, 'That's ok!' Or like when they called you sissy pants ? You should say, 'Thank you. I am glad you like my pants.' Or when they called you little baby chief ? Say something like, 'Yes, I am the chief's baby boy.' And smile! Don't run away unless they try to physically hurt you! Don't take what they say personally. They are only boys, just like you. Their words have no power over you, and they need to see that!"

Batista didn't say anything; he just stared at me, so I added one more piece of advice.
"I think that you should walk on the street again as soon as you can, but this time you will be ready for the challenge. You will not run away. When they throw their silly words at you, remember! You don't have to take them personally! Just smile and say, 'That's ok!' or if you can think of something else, say it. Don't run. Wait a few minutes and see what happens. If they speak again, repeat what you said. Then walk on down the street slowly like you have some place to go and you are not afraid."

"Will you go with me?" Batista asked.

"No," I said, "if I go with you, even if they can't see me, you will not overcome your fear of their silly words." Batista looked worried so I added, "When you come back from facing this challenge, I want you to find me right away because I will want to know how you handled this challenge, what you said, and. of course, I will be very proud of you. But more important, you will be proud of you!"

Batista nodded and I patted his shoulder. "I need to take a shower, now," I said. "Do you know how long it has been

78

since I took a hot shower?"

"How long?" said Batista.

"Three months!" I said.

"Wow," said Batista and he pulled away from me laughing and holding his nose. "You must really need a shower!" And then he ran out of the room, still laughing.

I looked through the clothes in my closet and dresser for things that had been a little big on me before I left; there wasn't much that would still fit me, but my mother had said we would go shopping for new clothes soon, and I was very much looking forward to that. I knew she would choose many of my clothes so they would be just like my brothers', so we could dress uniform for church and other social events, but sometimes she let me pick out a few things that were different from theirs. Those were the shirts and pants and ties that I really liked the best; I wore those when we had adult visitors with whom I could sit and talk.

I carried a white shirt and navy pants down the hall with me as I headed for the bathroom. The laundresses were bringing clean clothes back from the washroom to hang up in our closets or place, neatly folded, in our dressers, but there were also many other people in the hall that I didn't recognize. There were two women wearing long bright dresses and headwraps sitting on the floor in the corner near the door to my Daddy's office, and right next to them was a tall, very skinny, young man in black shorts and a baggy white T-shirt, leaning against the wall. My father's office door was closed, but I could hear him speaking in his usual careful way behind it. Occasionally someone else in the room muttered a monsyllable, but it was the rhythm of my Daddy's voice that dominated. I had missed him very much.

After my shower, I put on my clothes and walked barefoot back to my room. By now the two women were gone, as well as the skinny, young man, but three more people were waiting outside my Daddy's door. I sighed. This meant I wouldn't get to talk with him until maybe after our supper, and maybe not even then, but this was the life of a chief and his family. Responsibility to the people of our tribe came before everything else, and my Daddy's days were very full. Sometimes he was away working with the high government officials, and that meant that the tribal members who came to get his advice or help would have to wait for hours or even days to see him, but if they were patient, they would eventually get an answer from him.

You may wonder what kinds of problems they brought to him, but the only answer I can give you is that their problems were as many and varied as the people themselves. Sometimes he had to settle a dispute; I had witnessed this several times, but the procedure was always the same: first he listened to all sides, and then he gave his judgment. He had told me many times that the listening was the most important part, and although I had always been a good listener, I now made a conscious effort to listen even more carefully. "And," said my Daddy, "you must listen not only to what each person says, you must listen to what he doesn't say. In this way you will know many things, like who might not be telling the truth or what is being concealed. This takes practice!"

Often people came to my Daddy because they had a plan or a dream, but they didn't have the means to go after it; it might be more education or starting a business, and if he thought their dream was worthwhile and would benefit not only them, but the rest of the Lou tribe, he would provide the money. If it was schooling they wanted, he insisted that their grades were sent to him regularly, and they knew that if they weren't doing exemplary work for their teachers, he would stop paying for their education. If they were starting a business, he would go personally to inspect their premises when he could or even send someone they didn't know as a "customer" who would report back to him how well they were doing. I knew that my Daddy would want to help Sebastian, and I was eager to tell him about my brother's dream.

If there was anything about being my Daddy's second son that I disliked, it was this: that I would not have the same opportunity to lead our people as my brother Bazia would. And the irony of this was that my older brother didn't seem to care about this part of being a chief. Our Daddy had sometimes asked him if he wanted to stay in the office and listen to a dispute or help someone plan his dream, but Bazia always said he had schoolwork to do, the one excuse which Daddy would accept as valid. And I knew that this wasn't always the truth.

I didn't tell Daddy about my brother's deceit; it was not my place to take responsibility for Bazia's actions or decisions. They were his, and the consequences would be his as well. There were many times when I longed to be a witness to what was going on in the office, but I was only allowed to stay on rare occasions. That was why I spent so much time talking to my Daddy whenever he was not busy. He didn't mind sharing his wisdom with me then; he just didn't want our tribe to be confused by expecting me to be their chief someday.

Our evening meal on the day of my homecoming was very special: all of my favorite dishes, especially sweet potatoes,

81

were served, and it was good to sit there surrounded by my family who seemed to keep looking at me with a kind of wonder. I knew I was taller and stronger, but their studying glances made me speculate that there was something more showing in my face or in my behavior. Perhaps what I experienced on my "summer vacation" showed in other ways, but I was unable to see them myself.

My mother reminded me that as soon as we ate breakfast the next day, she expected me to be ready to shop for a whole new wardrobe, and I said I would be ready and was looking forward to it. Ireni asked if she could come, too, but my mother shook her head. "I bought you new clothes for school just last week," she said. "You have more than enough." Ireni pouted for the rest of the meal, pushing her food around her plate with her fork but not eating, and I smiled to myself. Obviously my sister had never experienced the pangs of hunger as I had.

After supper, the whole family went into the parlor where some visitors were already waiting. My siblings stayed only as long as they had to, and then, one by one, they went off with other children close to their age. I noticed that my older brother was still hanging around with the same two boys he had been following for years. He seemed to assert himself a little more now with them, reminding them that he was the chief's son whenever he wanted to get his way, but they were still very influential in his choices, and despite his parading his position, he was still very much their little puppy.

I talked with as many people as I could, but it had been a long day for me, and I was very eager to sleep in my sweet, clean, soft bed, so I left the gathering a little earlier than usual. I nodded to both of my parents as I left the room, and my mother reminded me again about the shopping which made me smile. Shopping for new clothes was one of the few interests we shared.

I yawned as I walked down the hall to my room. It would be a good night, sleeping alone in my very familiar bed rather than on the floor, I thought as I opened my door.

My room was dark which surprised me as the maids usually turned on the table lamps in the evening. I walked cautiously toward my bedside lamp to turn it on, fearing I would bump into furniture since I had been away from this room for so long that it was no longer familiar to me. There was a low rumbling sound coming from the bed, and I paused. It was the sound of snoring! Someone was already sleeping in my bed!

Chapter Eight: Still Different from the Rest

It was incredibly ironic that on my first night back home after a whole summer of sleeping on a grass mat over a dirt floor in a cinderblock house, I was once again in my own room but NOT in my own bed. I was able to slide one pillow off the edge of the mattress without disturbing my guest, and after putting on clean pajamas, I curled up in a corner of the room, out of the way of my roommate's feet. It was warm and I didn't need any covers, but it was definitely not the night's rest I had been looking forward to all day.

It could have been amusing, and I tried to think of it that way, but it wasn't easy. I had been looking forward to clean sheets, fluffy pillows, and a cushioned surface under my body, but that was not to be. To add to my woes, the guest in my bed began to snore, so I lay on my back and looked up at the ceiling, making plans for the next day.

83

One thing was certain: tomrrow I would make sure that I was sitting on my bed by the middle of the afternoon, probably around three o'clock, reserving what was really mine, but which was open for the use of any member of our tribe who was here to solicit my Daddy's advice or help. I struggled to find a comfortable position, which wasn't as difficult now as it had been before my summer vacation, and then I tried to speculate which of the visitors was sleeping in my bed. It wasn't completely dark, so I could see that his feet hung slightly over the end of the mattress; he was probably the tall, skinny, young man I had seen earlier in the hall. Then my thoughts turned to wonder what he was seeking, and as I pondered the possibilities, I fell asleep.

The next morning I woke late to find my guest had already departed; in the room where breakfast was served, I did notice that the tall skinny young man seemed to be avoiding me, but that might mean anything. I didn't blame him for taking my comfortable bed on my first night home; this was not a new event in my life. It was understood that if a tribal member came to seek my Daddy's advice or assistance, he or she would be able to eat and sleep in our house until a plan had been formed. And this could take as long as a week, especially if there were many people waiting to talk to the chief.

I sighed; this situation was not ideal, but it was like anything else, a matter of give and take. On the one hand, I was a fortunate child: I lived under my Daddy's umbrella. I never lacked for anything material, such as food, shelter, or nice clothes. I attended the best school in Khartoum. We had drivers to bring us anywhere we wanted to go. And I had the freedom to be myself.

On the other hand, as the son of the chief, I had to share

what I had with the rest of my tribe, including my bedroom should it be required. It was this responsibility that had been part of my thinking and training since I was very young, and it did me no good to resent it: this was the trade-off for my life in a privileged class. Even when I was very old, and a new generation had taken on the responsibility of leading our tribe, many would still come to me for advice and assistance, even though I was the second son. I knew this because people still traveled to the little village of Bazia not far from Khartoum where my Grandpop, my Daddy's daddy, lived in a small but comfortable house.

Thinking about this helped me decide what I should do when I returned from shopping with my mother; I would visit my Grandpop whom I had not even been able to bid good-bye before I was whisked off to live in a distant village for the summer. The day looked even brighter as I thought about this plan.

I was drinking hot tea as I finished my breakfast of fruit and a roll when my mother came to the door of the dining room, "Are you ready, Toni?" she said.

I quickly gulped down the rest of my tea and brought the roll with me, "Yes, I am ready!" I said, and we hurried out to the car. Buying a whole new wardrobe would certainly take away the disappointment of having slept on the floor last night!

We drove into the city and the driver let us out in the district where the best stores were. Our first stop was for shoes; my mother was surprised to discover that my feet were almost two sizes larger, but this change was no shock to me. I knew how much my old shoes had pinched my toes which was why I had switched to sandals. She bought me three new pairs of dress shoes, brown, black, and a very nice silver grey snakeskin. I liked that pair the best because they were different from the ordinary and people were bound to comment on them.

We walked two blocks down the street to our usual tailor, and once again my mother was amazed when he measured me. I had grown two inches taller, most of which seemed to be in my legs, and my chest was also much broader. Mother sat on a dainty chair in the shop, sipping tea from a China cup, while I stood on a platform in the center, and the tailor measured and remeasured my body.

His assistant popped out of the back room many times to show my mother fabric samples. She chose the usual grey flannel, fine quality, but nondescript, some black serge, navy rayon and tan linen as well, but she rejected a particularly nice grey and black pinstripe rayon which I thought would go especially well with my new snakeskin shoes, so I called out to her as the assistant began to return the bolt to the storage area, "Mother, do I have any of my birthday money still in the bank?" Mother raised her eyebrows and nodded, so I continued, "I would really like a suit made from that stripe. With a vest!"

She studied the fabric and then she studied me.

"I promise," I said, "not to wear it to church, just to be different."

She studied me some more.

"I promise," I said again. "That suit would look so nice with my new grey shoes."
She hesitated.

"Please?" I begged.

"Ok," said my mother, "I guess you are old enough to have some clothes that are not like everyone else's. I bought your brother a few things last week that were different from yours, Ireni's , and Batista's, so he could go into the offices in Khartoum with your father, and look like a young gentleman, not a child in a uniform. But you better keep your promise!"

I nodded eagerly, and the assistant added the bolt of cloth to the pile from which my new clothes would be made. My mother gave her final instructions to the tailor, signed an order for the work to be done, and asked that two of the suits , the black and the pinstripe, be finished as soon as possible. The tailor promised them for the following week.

From there we went to other shops and bought socks, underwear, shirts, two belts,
and three new pairs of pajamas. My waist had not grown so I could still wear the shorts and T-shirts I owned if I wanted to play in a rough and tumble way, but my mother knew that those occasions had always been rare. I had never been a child to ruin my clothes by running around, climbing walls or trees, or falling into mud puddles; in fact, it was this calmness in my behavior that was one reason that she would say, "You are not my child."

On the drive home, she looked at me and commented, "You know, I let your brother Bazia select two suits that were different from those he would wear to church, but he had a very hard time deciding what to pick. In the end, he chose a light brown linen, almost the same as the tan I had already selected, , and a darker shade of grey, also a flannel, but he really found making the decision difficult. He asked me several times what I liked, but I refused to

87

advise him. He even asked the tailor who was happy to recommend the light brown." She paused and looked out of the window for a while, and then turned back to me, "Perhaps," she said, "your father is right, and you are more my child than I realized."

I hoped that she would go on to explain what she meant, but it would be many years before I would know the story about my mother that made her understand how much I was her child. I wanted to know then, and I wanted to question her, but I knew it was not my right as her son to know her private thoughts unless she wanted to share them with me. As we pulled up in front of the house, I turned to her and said, "Thank you, Mother, for the new clothes. They are very fine. And I will not forget my promise."

As soon as I got out of the car, I said goodbye to her and dashed off to the dining room; by now, lunch was being served, and if I was going to see my Grandpop, I would need a sandwich for the ride so I could return by three and reserve my bed. In the dining room, I put some slices of cold chicken between two pieces of bread, doused the sandwich with hot sauce, and wrapped it in a napkin.

I ran back to the garage just as the driver was parking the car which had taken my mother and me into Khartoum. "Samuel," I said, "I need you to drive me to Bazia!"

Samuel laughed, "Bazia," he said, "has gone into Khartoum to visit his friends!"

I knew this game: it was one we often played when we were using the word *Bazia*. You see, this word is not just my family's name or the name of my older brother; it is the name of our original village and also the village of my

Grandpop as well. Even people in the tribe or in our own family would be confused by what was meant when you said Bazia , and the servants and I frequently made little jokes of misunderstanding about it. So when Samuel misunderstood me on purpose, I laughed, and said, "No, no, I don't mean young Bazia; I mean old Bazia!"

"Okay," said Samuel with a wink. "I am glad that you cleared that up! Hop in!"

The village of Bazia where my Grandpop, also called Bazia, lived was about three miles from Khartoum, and I could have walked but it would have taken me over an hour to get there. I would also have been tired and sweaty when I arrived, a condition of which I am not especially fond.

"Do you want me to drive you back after your visit?" Samuel looked at me in the rear view mirror.

"That would be good," I said. "I need to be home by three."

"Ah," said Samuel, nodding, "Your Daddy's house is very full right now, isn't it?"

"As it should be," I replied. It would not do to have him think I was complaining. I was well aware of how much the servants talked about our family and our personal matters. This wasn't something we could stop, but we all knew that getting too familiar with servants could lead to trouble. I was probably more likely to talk with them than my brothers or sister; after all, they were people, too and I knew they had feelings and opinions just like I did, but I did have to be very careful about what I said to them because it was bound to be repeated, and occasionally, exaggerated or altered in a way that reflected poorly on my

89

Daddy. But I was always kind and polite to them.

This was not always the case with my older brother or Ireni. Ireni had a terrible temper and on more than one occasion, I had heard her yelling at a laundress about the "terrible wrinkles" in a dress or skirt. This was very unfair of her because I knew how the wrinkles had gotten there: Ireni always selected her clothes by what I called the grab and toss method: she would stand in front of her wardrobe and dresser and pull out item after item until something struck her fancy. The rejects were thrown on the bed or the floor for the servants to hang back up when she left the room. I had even seen her walk on these perfectly ironed clothes on her way out; no wonder some of them became "terribly wrinkled".

My older brother tended to ignore the servants, like they were mobile furniture or robots to whom he could issue commands whenever he liked. They were not offended; they really didn't expect anything better from him, but there was one particular servant whom he treated far more rudely than she deserved.

This was Christiana, a kitchen maid who was also given jobs of cleaning around the house between meals. She was quite young, only a few years older than Young Mr. Bazia, as he was usually called, and for some reason, she had a crush on him. I knew this because if he was sitting in the dining room eating his breakfast, she would come into the room frequently and hover nearby. If his coffee cup was empty, she hurried to refill it. When he dropped his napkin or a piece of silverware, she dashed off and brought him a new one. In fact, I was quite dismayed one day to see him drop first his spoon, then his fork, and finally his napkin, on the floor on purpose so that Christiana was waiting on him constantly. What he was doing was taking advantage of her feelings for him, and it bothered me.

His worst treatment of her was something I witnessed quite by accident. It was late one afternoon and my brother was sitting in the living room alone. I was there, too, reading the newspaper, but he was waiting for a driver. He seemed especially impatient that day, tapping his fingers on his knee or running them down the crease in his pantleg. He would lean back and cross one leg over his knee as if to relax, but in a few minutes, he would uncross his legs, and lean forward.

Suddenly Christiana came into the room; she was carrying a tall stack of clean folded towels, and she was obviously headed for the bathrooms. She didn't notice my brother as she walked straight across the room toward the hall, but he noticed her.

"Christiana," he said, a little sharply. "Go to the garage and tell Samuel I expect him to bring my ride around right now!"

Christiana was so startled that she jumped a little, and the top two towels fell off the stack onto the floor. She was flustered now, and she bent over to pick up the two towels, but my brother snapped at her, "Never mind those! Go tell Samuel to come right now!"

The girl stared at him, dropped all of the towels, and burst into tears. She obviously didn't know what she should do; here was Young Mr. Bazia telling her to fetch him a car, but she was also supposed to be restocking the towels in the bathrooms. No matter what she did, somebody was going to be angry with her.

91

My brother was totally unaware of the dilemma she was in, nor did he care. "Well," he continued, "what are you standing there for? Get going!"

Christiana wiped the tears off her face and walked out the front door. My brother stood up and went to the window to watch. "Good," he said, "she's headed toward the garage. Finally I can leave."

In the few minutes that it took for the car to arrive, I thought seriously about saying something to my brother about his treatment of the maid. He seemed totally oblivious to her feelings about him as well as how he had created a problem for her by interfering in her household duties. He simply didn't look at other people as if they had the same feelings or problems that he had; to his way of thinking, the world was here to meet his needs, but he was under no obligation to consider theirs.

I knew that speaking to him, even mildly about his attitude and his actions, would be a complete waste of time. In fact, I suspected he might even misinterpret my protection of the maid, and make some rude comment about my being soft on the servants. I had seen him react to my Daddy's criticism, so I was sure that he wouldn't understand and that my words would not change him. I said nothing.

The driver drove up in front and Christiana came back into the room. Without even a thank you, Young Mr. Bazia charged out the doorway and got into the car. The maid stood for a few minutes by the window and stared after him, her feelings for him revealed in her eyes and her sad, sad mouth. Then she turned and began to pick up the towels, refolding them in a neat stack.

"He doesn't see you," I said.

"What?" Christiana apparently hadn't realized that I was there on the other side of the room, behind my newspaper.

"He doesn't even see you," I repeated, lowering the paper. "He doesn't see you, and he doesn't know how you feel about him. He doesn't understand such feelings, but that doesn't mean you are bad to feel them. Your heart is a kind one, and his, well, he doesn't understand. It isn't your fault, but there is nothing to be done."

"I know, " she said sadly, "I am only a servant and he is the chief's son. I have known from the beginning that it was hopeless, but I cannot seem to stop how I feel."

"In time," I said, "you will see him for who he really is, and then even your kind heart will cease to care so much. Be patient with yourself, and try to be happy. Your kind heart will surely find another man who will care for you as well." Christiana nodded; her eyes were filling up again with tears.

"Remember," I added, " he doesn't treat you this way to be cruel; he simply doesn't see you at all. Try not to take it personally. He treats everyone this way. If you watch him, you will see this."

Again the maid wiped her eyes, and then she finished folding and stacking the towels. She picked up the pile and headed toward the bathrooms.

I never had occasion to speak with her again, but over the next few months, I noticed that she did indeed follow my advice. She watched my brother carefully and she listened when he was rude or demanding with the other servants.

93

In time, I hoped that she would be able to forget him. But life sometimes is very cruel, especially when the heart becomes involved.

Chapter Nine: The Big Difference

As the car got closer to my Grandpop's house, I told my driver to let me off away from the end of the drive, and for him to go on, into the village to turn around. I would walk the short distance from there to my Grandpop's because I wanted to surprise him. I was really looking forward to this reunion.

Now you may be wondering at this point why, if I am so eager and excited to see my Grandpop, I have not really talked much about him before. I think it is time I explained a very important part of how my philosophy works for me, and maybe you can benefit from this understanding. What it all comes down to is that the big difference between me and most other people that I know is that I don't go by emotion. What does this mean?

It means that I don't let my emotions run my life. And I have been living my life this way for as long as I can remember.

This is the habit that has set me apart from my parents and my siblings, the practice that has made them say from time to time, "Ah, Toni is different. That chocolate boy may look sweet, but he has no heart."

Or sometimes they use different words, like "Toni has a cold heart." But nothing could be further from the truth. I have a heart, just like you, and like them, and I feel things deeply. I feel pain and pleasure, sadness and joy, admiration, anger, despair, contentment, frustration, confusion, hope, the list goes on and on. I am not a robot or a machine. I am a human being, just like you. But here is the difference: when I feel an emotion, no matter what it is, I do not let it control my behavior. First, before I do anything at all, I think.

Remember back in Chapter One when I told a little story about my older brother bumping into a table as he walked through a room? How when he did that and his leg hurt from the collision, he would kick the table and probably hurt his foot as well? That is a perfect example of how going by emotion can make your life more difficult. If you look at this incident, step by step, you can see how going by emotion is really a trap.

Step One: My brother bumps into the table.
Step Two: His leg hurts as a result of the collision.
Step Three: The pain makes him angry.
Step Four: Being angry makes him want to strike back.
Step Five: He kicks the table.
Step Six: He injures his foot.

Now the really surprising thing about this incident is that eventually, my brother stops striking out at inanimate objects. Step Six seems to cause him to think, just a little bit maybe, and yes, he would probably yell or swear or protest this second injury to himself in some way, but he does stop making the situation worse. Step Seven would probably be that he leaves the room, yelling and complaining about his injured leg and his sore foot, still going by emotion, but, at least, not quite so foolishly.

So where does the problem of hitting the table get worse? It gets worse right after Step Four, when he feels like striking back, and so, takes Step Five and kicks the table. What needs to happen to change the way my brother reacts is that he needs to think about his emotional reaction and decide what to do that will not create further problems for him, or anyone else for that matter. He could move the table out of his way so that he won't run into it again. He could slow down and move more cautiously so he won't run into things in the next room. Both of these solutions are not emotional; they are thoughtful. They make sense and they don't lead to further damage or more upsetting emotions.

So when members of my family accused me of having a cold heart or, even worse, no heart at all, it was because they didn't understand me. They thought I didn't go by emotion because I didn't *have* emotions. They didn't understand that I used thought instead of emotion to choose my actions, but my Grandpop did.

And that was why when I was sent away for the summer vacation, I missed my Grandpop more than anyone else. Everyone needs to have a person who knows him for who he (or she) truly is inside, and for me, that person was my Grandpop. In fact, that was the reason why I tried very hard not to think about him when I was sent away. I knew that if I did think about him, I would feel such sadness that I couldn't see him that I might not be able to think in an unemotional way about what I needed to do when I was living with that strange and difficult family. I realized that I would feel more loneliness than I had ever experienced before, and loneliness is a very powerful emotion. It can drain your strength and make you depressed, so on the first night that I lay down on the grass mat in the boys' room, when the sounds of my new brothers' soft breathing told me that they were asleep, I thought about my Grandpop and I cried. I cried very hard but as quietly as I could, and fortunately my sobs woke no one. Then, before I fell asleep, I took one more step to prevent myself from being hurt by this loneliness and longing over and over again: I pictured my Grandpop sitting in the sunshine in front of his house, smiling and waiting for me to come home. I had no doubt that my parents would come and bring me back home eventually, and I knew my Grandpop would in no way blame me for going away; he would understand that this was some kind of test or punishment devised by my Daddy. I knew he would be waiting to see his little chocolate boy as eagerly as I always rushed to talk with him, but that I wouldn't see him for a long time. I put my happy picture of his smiling face in a box inside my head, I closed the lid, and I told myself I wouldn't open the box again until I was back home.

Now I really don't know where I got the idea to do this; perhaps God was helping me deal with a pain which was so big that I couldn't handle it any other way, but I did know that this was the right thing to do. I had already been practicing the art of thinking rather than going by emotion for so long that I knew very strong emotions need special handling. I had learned, for example, that rage (extreme anger) was an emotion which could take over your behavior so quickly that you didn't have a lot of time to think about what to do. In fact, it is a theory of mine that anger was the first emotion that I learned not to go by. And strangely enough, I can thank my older brother for this practice.

I don't know why this is so, but everyone I have ever met who was not the first child born in a family, but one of the younger siblings, has stories to tell about being teased and tortured by the oldest child. It is as if that first child must immediately establish power over the new arrival, thus making sure that he or she, as first born, remains the most important child, receives the most attention, and gets his or her way more often. Parents often tell the oldest, "Take care of your little brother (or sister). Share your toys. Be nice to him (or her)," but in reality, when they are not watching closely or sometimes even when they are nearby, the oldest child teases or aggravates the younger until the younger child loses control and begins to hit, cry, or express his frustration in some other way. At this point, the first child looks innocent and surprised, as if to say, I didn't do anything!, and the younger child is whisked away for a nap because he obviously needs it.

My older brother Bazia was no exception to this situation; he delighted in making faces at me that frightened me until I cried, or he would snatch away my favorite plaything and hold it just out of my reach until I screamed (and then put it on the floor in front of me when my parents or a servant came to investigate the commotion). Sometimes he mumbled insults or made fun of me when I made a mistake in speech. He had a million ways to make me lose control. And when I did, he won, and I was removed from the society of adults until I could act less like a baby.

But somewhere, somehow, I realized what was going on. I saw, for a brief moment, that although I couldn't stop him from doing these very annoying things to me, and I couldn't stop feeling the anger that they produced, I could fight back another way besides crying or throwing something at him. I could smile at him, and say "It's okay."

The first time I did that, his face was a study in surprise and shock. He stared at me. He couldn't believe it. Here he was, dangling my favorite toy of the week, a little red monkey with a yellow hat, over my head where I couldn't get it, and I was sitting on the floor, smiling at him calmly and saying, "It's okay."

When he waved the monkey under my nose, I continued to smile and didn't try to grab it. He pretended to rip an arm off the monkey, but I didn't react. He threw the monkey up in the air where it hit the ceiling and fell back down in front of me. I smiled and said, "Okay." He stared at me some more and then reacted to his own emotions of frustration by throwing the monkey at me and stomping out of the room.

At this disturbance, my mother looked up from her book at him. "What's going on, Bazia?" she asked, but my brother, who was halfway down the hall, had nothing to say. She looked at me, and I smiled back. "It's okay," I said, and I knew it really was. I had won.

This was the first of many victories in my life achieved because I didn't use my emotions to make my decisions. If you look back at the previous chapters, especially my account of the three months spent in that distant village with a family of strangers, you will see that my habit of thinking was what saved me from a miserable experience. When my parents drove away and left me there, like any other child, I was confused and felt like they were rejecting me, even abandoning me, but unlike another child, I didn't cry, rage, or protest the situation because I knew this would have done me no good, and it would have created a lasting impression with my new family that I was spoiled willful brat from a privileged home who acted like a baby when he didn't get his way.

Instead, I focused my attention on understanding the new family with whom I was now living, and right away I decided that I would turn my thoughts toward setting an example of cooperation and kindness that they might copy. I thought that working toward this goal would make my summer interesting and keep me from feeling sorry for myself, and I was right. And now, as I walked up the little road toward my Grandpop's house, I could hardly wait to tell him how well my plan had worked.

At a bend in the road, I slowed down and moved close to the bushes on the side because if my Grandpop was outside, as he often was, he would see me as soon as I came around this little curve. I moved very slowly, almost peeking around the corner toward the front of his house, and, yes, there he was, sitting in the sunshine, just as he often did in the early afternoon right after lunch. But he didn't see me because he was dozing.

I stood in the warm sunshine and waited. This was just how I had pictured him when I put him in a box in my mind three months before. I could wait a little longer.

Suddenly a fly began to buzz around my Grandpop's balding head. First it landed on his nose, and without opening his eyes, he brushed it away with his hand. Then the fly landed boldly on the bare strip of skin on the top of his head, like it was a landing strip between the two rows of vegetation formed by the greying curls of his hair on both sides. Grandpop snorted, lifted both hands to brush away the fly, and opened his eyes.

"Chocolate Boy," he cried with delight, "I was just dreaming about you! And here you are!"
He reached out and clasped both my arms. "Sit down here with me on the step and tell me about your summer."

And so, for the next hour, I did.

Chapter Ten: The Tribe Called The Lou

100

About an hour later, I was sitting at my Grandpop's kitchen table where I watched the steaming tea water darken in my glass until it was the strength I preferred and then I fished out the teabag with my long spoon. My Grandpop's teabag, its dark green Kenya tea label still attached, already lay on a little saucer between us on the table, so I put my teabag beside it. Then I added sugar to the hot tea, about three heaping spoonfuls as I liked my tea hot, strong, and sweet. My Grandpop's was even sweeter, but not so concentrated. He had told me before I left for the summer that he believed as one got older, one needed less caffeine because often with age came sleeping disturbances.

"How well are you sleeping at night, Grandpop?" I asked politely.

"Okay," he said, " but I often wake up just after midnight and then I cannot sleep again for an hour or so. I have tried to avoid falling asleep after lunch, but if I sit down outside in the sunshine, like today, you see what happens!" Grandpop chuckled. "It would seem that I need shorter sleeps throughout the day and night. I remember my father and my grandfather were both the same as they aged. It doesn't mean anything is wrong, Toni, so don't worry about me."

I nodded at my Grandpop's answer and for a while, we sat in silence and drank our tea. "Your great-great grandfather, the Bazia whom you love to hear about, was a very unusual man," he began. I settled back in my chair: this was a story I had been hearing for so long that it had become a comfortable ritual in my life. It always made me feel very close to the long line of chiefs from whom I was descended because I was very proud to have the family name of Bazia.

101

"One story I heard about this Bazia," my Grandpop went on, "was that as he got older, he refused to eat the flesh of animals. He ate only vegetables, especially beans and peanuts and rice, and although many of the people of his tribe looked at him and shook their heads, saying he would not make old bones on such a diet, they were wrong. In fact, he lived to be in his eighties and was, in many ways, healthier and more active than men much younger, men who dined regularly on the flesh of antelope and zebra and other wild animals they killed." My Grandpop shook his head and sipped some tea.

"I don't intend to copy his diet," Grandpop grinned and patted his small but slightly protruding belly, "I do like my meat."

"Did he do this to improve his health?" I asked. I could have guessed at the answer from what I already knew about my great-great-grandfather, but this was a new piece of information and I wanted to know what my Grandpop had been told.

"No, not for his health," Grandpop shook his head, "but for the health of the animals. He would often take long walks out into the bush and sit there silently, watching the great herds run and feed and fight over females and mate. He especially liked to watch the newborn calves as they played with each other, almost like human children play tag. I have seen this, too. The youngsters butt each other, just in fun, and then dash off, hoping the others will chase them which, of course, they often do."

"I have not seen this," I said.

"You would have to walk a long way into the bush to see

102

this now," Grandpop shook his head again, "because there are no more large herds of game in Sudan. I am afraid we have eaten most of them."

"Then that early Bazia was right?" I asked.

"Yes, but even more, he said these animals were not so different from us, that they had feelings, families, even the same right to life. He was a gentle man."

I heard the break in the word and I knew my Grandpop did not mean that this long-ago Bazia had been a dignified man, a man of education and class, a gentleman as the British would say. I knew he was referring to my ancestor's inherent kindness and mercy toward all living things. And since I knew the most important story about my ancestor, this did not surprise me.

"You do remember, Toni," continued my Grandpop, "because I know I have told this part many times, that your great-great-grandfather Bazia saved our tribe of Lou from extinction?"

"Yes, but tell me again, " I said.

"Well, at the time that this Bazia was chief of the Lou, our tribe lived perhaps a hundred or more miles away from here to the east. We lived very much as we still do, farming, raising some cattle, trading with our neighbors, and, of course, we also hunted back then. As a tribe, we were well known in Sudan as being highly intelligent and wise." My Grandpop was silent for a few minutes and then went on, "But this didn't prevent us from having our share of tragedy."

Now we were coming to the part I knew so well that I

103

could echo my Grandpop's words, but I stayed silent and listened to his voice. I felt very much at home now, and that was a very good feeling, indeed.

"Perhaps it was because of our reputation as intelligent, wise people that we gained the attention of another tribe. If I once knew the name of that tribe, I have forgotten it, but in any case, as it turned out, it would do no good to try to discover who they were. It would make no difference now. I do remember that they had a reputation as fierce warriors. In fact, one group of their tribe had overcome another small tribe not far from us, killed most of their men, and taken their women for their own. That village now belonged to them, but they were a tribe who needed even more space, so the next people they looked at for a future target was our tribe, the Lou."

"They had the lust for conquest," I said, and my Grandpop nodded.

"Yes," he said, "they wanted to take over our village in much the same way. We were few in numbers, especially in skilled warriors, but our land was rich, and our women, then as now, were very beautiful. In fact, it is entirely possible they hoped to breed smarter children through mingling their blood with ours. But this is only something my father told me."

A wind-up clock in the parlor chimed twice, and I remembered that my driver would be coming to get me pretty soon. This very familiar story, however, was very comforting, and I wanted to hear it all, once again.

"Then something very unusual happened." My Grandpop looked at me as he went on, "This unusual thing was also very fortunate for us. One day, a member of that tribe of

104

fierce warriors came to our village to trade for some cattle. He brought with him his latest wife who had once been a member of the small tribe they had conquered. She was very young and beautiful. My father said the warrior treated her like a beast of burden because she was carrying a large basket filled with items of jewelry to trade for cows, but it is also possible he brought her along to show her off and brag a little in front of our tribe. She was also pregnant and very close to having the child, and when they arrived in our village, she complained of feeling faint and weak."

"Your great-great-grandfather immediately saw her distress and called for his first wife to help. He ordered that this young woman be taken inside a hut and there allowed to lie down. She would be offered water and fruit, or a meal if she so desired, and the fierce warrior, although he scowled and argued, could not say no for fear of losing the woman as well as the unborn child."

"While the young wife rested in the hut, the fierce warrior walked around our ancestral village. He examined the shaky palisade fence that kept wild animals out of the gardens. He looked at all of our men of fighting age, many of whom were resting in the shade of large trees. He also looked at any young woman who walked by, and his looks were filled with desire. He smiled a lot. Then he traded the items in the basket for five cows."

"Our ancestor, the Bazia, offered him fruit and water as well, and the warrior took it. He hardly thanked your great-great-grandfather but acted as if this courtesy was only his due. The Bazia later said that this man's attitude only confirmed what his wife later told him."

"As it was growing dark, the warrior called his young wife

from the hut, and the two of them left the village, guiding the cows in front of them with a stick and saying they needed to return to their home for the night. Bazia followed them a way down the trail and then stood waving at them and grinning foolishly as he watched them walk out of sight. Then he hurried back to the village."

"There his first wife told him what he already suspected. The young pregnant woman had revealed that this visit had very little to do with trading for cattle, but was a spy mission from that other tribe of warriors who already had it in their minds to conquer our ancestral village."

"The Bazia's wife also told him that the young woman had wept when she told them about the other tribe's desire for our village, saying that this other tribe was very skilled in battle and without mercy. She said there were at least one hundred men who regularly practiced by fighting each other. She also said that they were planning to make their attack in about two weeks, long enough for our village to forget about this visit, but not so long that our village could build better fortifications if we had any suspicions of an attack. She promised that she would not tell her husband what she had revealed to us. She added that she wished us good fortune and was sorry to be the teller of such terrible news."

"Your great-great-grandfather wasted no time. He immediately called everyone into the center of the village for a meeting, and then, he told them the bad news."

"There was an immediate uproar, with much wailing and crying from the women, and angry shouts from the men who ran to their huts and brought out the knives, spears, and machetes they used to hunt or defend the village. Some of these items were badly in need of sharpening, but

106

the men sat down with whetstones and began the task. Some of younger men, those whose hearts go before their heads, decided that the Lou should attack this tribe of fierce warriors before they attacked our village. One hothead even offered to run after the visiting couple with his friends and kill them both before they returned home with the information about how vulnerable the Lou tribe was. 'They will think twice about attacking us then!' the young man said."

"'And if they come after us for revenge?' the Bazia said."

"'We will slaughter them!'"

"'And how many warriors do they have?'"

"'She said a hundred, but everyone knows that women exaggerate.'"

"'And how many warriors do we have? Please, will all our experienced warriors
stand so we can count you?' The Bazia lifted his hands in supplication to the men who were sharpening weapons."

"There was silence for a moment and the men all looked at each other. Then a few stood, and then a couple more until no more men got to their feet. Your great-great-grandfather counted those standing. There were fifteen."

"The women began wailing again, and soon all the babies were crying as well while the fifteen experienced warriors stood with their heads hanging in shame."

"The Bazia waved his hands in the air for silence. 'There is no need,' he said, 'for shame that we are not a tribe of fierce warriors who conquer our neighbors, loot their

107

villages, rape their women, and sell their children into slavery.' There was gasp when he said this, but once more he waved his hands, and all the people listened."

"'We must relocate,' the Bazia said. 'We must spend tonight going through all of our possessions and pack only those things that we can carry for some distance and will truly need when we come to the end of our journey. We must also provide for ourselves by harvesting all the fruits and vegetables we can and putting them in the three wagons we have. Then, in the morning, we must start what may be a very long journey. We will go west and look for a new place to build a new village.'"

"There was once more muttering among the younger men, and the hothead stood up again. 'We must fight,' he shouted. 'We cannot let them do this to us! We must fight to the death!'"

"'Whose death?' said the Bazia. 'Outnumbered by more than six to one, you will fight to your death, and when you lie bleeding out your life upon this land where we have always lived, who will defend your mother? Your sisters? Your ancient uncle? Who will prevent these others from selling your younger brothers into slavery? This is not the wisdom for which the Lou are known.'"

"The hothead looked around and urged some of his friends to stand beside him, but one took his arm and pulled him down on the ground again. He said nothing more."

"The Bazia urged everyone to do as he said, and he ordered the young men to pick everything edible in all the gardens and pack the produce into the wagons. The older men went to herd all of the cattle together and look them over, making sure they were fit for the journey. If one or more were too slow, they would be killed first and used to feed the village as they traveled."

"In the morning there was no need to call out to the people to rise and begin their search for a new home. They were all ready to go, packs on their backs or baskets on their heads. Those old people who were too ancient to walk were allowed to ride up on the drivers' seats of the wagons, and a young man was assigned the job of leading the animals harnessed to these vehicles. It was a clear warm day, promising to get hot, and the Bazia ordered that many buckets of water be carried on poles by the young men. Last in the line were ten of the fifteen men who claimed to be experienced warriors, in case the Lou tribe should be attacked from behind. The remaining five were scattered throughout the march, armed against the attack of a lion. The Bazia marched at the head of the line, his three wives behind him."

"It was a long journey, but in six weeks, the tribe of Lou arrived at a beautiful valley which appeared to have no inhabitants. On the advice of the Bazia, they all camped there for a week before beginning to build huts, hunt, or dig and plant. It would not do to offend a nearby tribe who already had a claim to this land, not after they had walked so far in search of a new home."

"But no one came to tell them to go away, so they stayed. And so the tribe of Lou survived and came to live here," my Grandpop swung his arm around him to include the present village, his house, and the few other houses scattered beyond.

I heard the honk of a car's horn, and I knew it was time to go home, home to claim my bed for a good sleep, home to learn more from my Daddy about being a good chief. "I will visit you again soon, Grandpop," I said as I ran out to waiting car.

Chapter Eleven: My Big Dream

I have told you about the importance of individual dreams along with my feeling that God put me (and everyone else, for that matter) on this planet for a reason, but I have not told you about my personal childhood dream.

My personal dream began when I was younger than the times I have already told you about; I was probably about six . This dream was the result of our first visit from some other family members who had traveled further than I had, but later this visit became an annual event, thus supplying me with fresh fuel every year for my dream.

Cousin Dominic was about my father's age, a married man who worked at the Sudanese Embassy in Washington, D.C. He had several children, also cousins of mine, close to my age, and when he returned on vacation every year with his family from the United States to Sudan, (for our nation was not divided when I was a child), he usually came to Khartoum and stayed with our family for several weeks.

He and my father would talk about politics both in Sudan and abroad, and I would often listen in, but even more exciting to me were the stories his children shared about their life in the United States of America, their schools, their friends, where they shopped, and how Americans lived. I would listen spellbound when they talked about life back "home", for although they, too, were Sudanese, they spent so much of the year in the United States that they no longer thought of Sudan as their homeland, and they frequently complained that they didn't really enjoy these annual treks back to Africa. They would have much preferred to stay in D.C. and spend their summer vacation with their American friends, as well as the children from other embassies all over the world. They seemed to find our lifestyle boring compared to theirs, especially when it came to technology and entertainment. In fact, if we hadn't had a satellite dish so they could keep up with their American television programs, their visits would have been one long session of listening to them whine.

But the satellite programs kept them from being too unhappy and for many hours of each day, I could always find one or more of these cousins who would be happy to watch television with me and explain the parts of the programs which I, not yet being fluent in English, couldn't understand. I wanted to watch everything from old war movies to documentaries about Hollywood film stars, not to mention all the sports competitions and news programs. I even watched the sitcoms and soap operas that my girl cousins were addicted to because it was especially interesting to me how different the lifestyles of Americans were from my own family's or the families of our servants and neighbors.

Every American family supposedly had a house in which they lived in without the infringement of relatives or another family sharing their space. They had at least one car and lots of electronic devices which did all their work for them, instead of the servants that cooked our meals, cleaned our floors, and washed our clothes for us. Their style of dress was more casual and the interaction between husbands and wives and parents and children less formal. Children even challenged the opinions and judgments of their parents, but the parents didn't seem to mind. And as soon as an American teenager reached the legal age, he (or she) got a driver's license and bought a car! In Sudan, only the wealthy owned cars and they always had a chauffeur. I never saw a traffic jam until I began watching American television, and it was amazing to me that there could be so many cars on a road that their movement would slow down to a crawl or even stop completely. Years later, as I drove along the Freeway in California, I was still amazed to be surrounded by so many vehicles.

Every summer brought a new type of program that enlightened me further about American lifestyles. The year I watched a lot of Westerns, I became convinced that there were almost as many horses in America as there were cars! Eventually someone informed me that these shows where cowboys herded cattle and fought each other in range wars or got revenge for attacks by Native Americans (called Indians at the time, which was certainly confusing since none of them came from India!) were primarily historical and not very accurate at that.
I watched shows about crime and law enforcement, typical American families and the problems they faced, and even got a glimpse of outer space as imagined by American writers of shows like Lost in Space or Star Trek , but the most consistent impression American television made on me was that this country called the United States seemed to offer all of its people many resources that were available to only the most privileged residents of Sudan, especially in their hospitals and from their physicians.

The summer I was sent to live with a poor family in a village was the one summer that I didn't see these cousins or wallow in hours and hours of television, building upon my dream of someday living in the United States of America, a dream I had revealed to my Daddy, my Grandpop, and the rest of my family. In fact, my dream was so strong that I spoke of it as a certainty. I will live there someday I told everyone, and although my siblings laughed while the adults raised skeptical eyebrows, I viewed my future life in America as an event which was just around the corner. I knew it would happen.

So when I returned home from my summer in the bush village, my biggest regret was missing that visit from my cousins. I tried watching some television programs by myself, but there was so much I didn't understand that I soon found other things to do. Besides, with the return to school and my studies, which I took very seriously, there wasn't much time to sit and watch images on a screen while I tried to puzzle out what the people were saying.

The rest of that year was fairly uneventful for me. I celebrated my tenth birthday on Christmas Day, an event which is always very meaningful for me. I kept my promise to my mother and she allowed me to occasionally wear outfits of clothing which were uniquely mine, although I was not able to do this for church or other places where our entire family was in the public view. I especially like getting dressed up for those rare occasions when my father would go to eat lunch or meet with other important men in Khartoum. My older brother Bazia often accompanied Daddy, but every once in a while, Daddy invited me to go with them. Rarer, but most precious, were the times when Young Bazia didn't go, and I went in his place. Daddy always made it clear that I was his second son, but I answered so well when the important men asked me questions about what I was learning in school or what I thought of a current issue that my Daddy smiled. I knew he was proud of me. My position in the family was only an accident of birth and since the tribe had been known to select a chief from the younger members of the chief's family, there was still hope for me, especially if Young Bazia continued to show so little interest in politics or the leadership of our tribe.

Perhaps this increased confidence, combined with what I was learning from American television, led me to make my next big mistake. It was also a result, I am certain, of my growing desire to help others. My experience in the village with my foster family had shown me the enormous pleasure one got from helping someone else solve his problems or fulfill his or her dreams. In fact, within a month of my homecoming, I had told my Daddy about Sebastian and his desire to stay in school so that he could acquire the skills he needed to open a store in Khartoum when he grew up rather than spend his life a farmer like his father. After all, it was not like my foster father didn't have younger sons, certainly one of whom would be eager to take over the family business!

My father smiled and nodded as I explained Sebastian's dream and the conflict between his father's goals for him and his own. "I must handle this very delicately, Toni," my Daddy said, "but you were right to tell me. It would be a good thing for this young man to stay in school and get an education so that he can go into business someday, and as chief of the Lou, it is my responsibility to make this possible."

My Daddy paused in thought for a moment and then went on, "But I cannot really force his father to let him stay in school. I must find a way for the man to think it was his own idea."

Daddy reached for a pen and some writing paper. "I will write to the school teacher with a proposal that will make it possible for several oldest sons in that village to continue in school."
As he wrote, my Daddy explained, "This letter to the school

114

teacher explains that I am establishing a scholarship award to be given to three boys in that village. Each recipient must be the oldest child in his family. He must be a good student. And he must have shown a genuine desire to complete the high school level of study. For each year that this student continues to attend school full time and successfully completes his program of studies, the head of his family will receive one hundred dollars in compensation for this child's contribution of work time in the family business, whatever that might be. And each applicant must write me a letter telling me why he wishes to continue his education. I am sure that we can use these letters to select the most appropriate candidates for the scholarships." Daddy smiled at me and I smiled back.

And within two weeks of sending off that letter to the school teacher, seven application letters had arrived! My Daddy and I read them together; I was able to spot Sebastian's at once because I recognized his large blocky writing. He wrote well, but his letter was definitely not the best. It actually fell somewhere in the middle in terms of correctness, but as my face fell, fearing that my foster brother would not receive the help he so desperately wanted and needed, my Daddy reassured me.

"I think, Toni," he said as he dropped the last letter into the pile between us, "I failed to anticipate how important continuing education might be to the young men of a small village. I think I will have to increase the number of scholarships from three..."and here Daddy paused and I held my breath, "to seven. That way, all of these fine young scholars can, if they apply themselves, graduate from high school."

"Thank you, Daddy," I said.

"I may look into doing something like this in another village, or two," Daddy went on. "It would be to the advantage of the entire tribe. All too often, young men from the bush come here asking to get an education or start a business, but because of circumstances like your brother Sebastian, they must spend as much as two years studying what they should have learned in their village schools before I can send them to college or university." Daddy sighed, "And for some, it is too late."

"Thank you, Daddy, " I said again.

So this uneventful year continued into the spring, or the end of the dry season. My brothers and sister and I went to school, we dressed in our uniforms for church, and each of us did whatever we each enjoyed when we had free time. Ireni seemed to spend most of her time painting her nails or her face, creating new hairdos, or trying on different combinations of clothes. Young Bazia hung out with his friends, while Batista followed them around like a puppy. He occasionally talked to me, but more and more I could see that he found my interests boring. I liked to talk to people and so I spent my free time with my Grandpop, my Daddy, or even the servants.

I had become especially interested in a servant family that lived almost next door to our house. Their little cottage was not as grand as our home, and it was, with only five rooms and seven people, definitely more crowded, but I liked to go there to visit when I got out of school. There was always something interesting going on, and they all seemed to like me. The mother, who was also one of our laundry maids, was often cooking something delicious when I dropped by and she always insisted that I sample the dish. I knew that they didn't have much to spare so when I could, I would bring them something I had bought in the

116

market, like a bag of rice or cornmeal. I didn't want to impose on their friendship.

So it was on a warm day near the end of April that I knocked on their door, my arms aching from carrying a five kilo sack of meal. At first there was no answer so I listened. It was very quiet. Perhaps, I thought, they had all gone out for the afternoon. But then, I heard a soft sobbing. I set down the bag of meal and waited a minute; the volume of the weeping increased. I knocked again, louder.

The mother came to the door. "Oh, Toni," she said in surprise. I could see that her eyes were red and swollen. "I am not cooking today," she went on. "I appreciate your gift of meal, but I don't think we can visit today." She wiped her eyes with her apron. "I'm really sorry."

"I don't want to intrude, " I said, "but please, what is the matter? Is there anything I can do to help?"

"I don't think so," she answered and then she swayed a little, as if she were going to fall down. I moved quickly to her side and caught her. Then, since I knew the house well, I walked with her leaning against me into the kitchen and helped her sit down. The sound of weeping which I had heard through the door was much louder now and I could see at least one source because the oldest daughter, Adella, was already seated at the kitchen table, her face in her hands. She was crying hard.

"Please, "I said to the daughter, "will you help your mother? I think she needs a glass of water."

Adella raised her head; her eyes,too, were red and swollen and tears were still streaming down her face, but she hurried to the cupboard, got a glass, and filled it with cold water from the kitchen tap. Then she handed it to her mother who said, "Thank you."

I stood by the doorway, not knowing what to do next. Technically, I had forced my way into their home; I had not been invited to enter, but as I stood there, the mother took a deep breath and said, "Please sit down, Toni. I think you will find out what is happening soon enough so I might as well tell you." She drank some of the water and then continued,"My youngest, my son, David, is going to die."

"David?" I was shocked. I knew the whole family, father, mother, and five children, four girls and their one young son. I had seen David playing ball outside in the road only the week before. He had looked healthy enough then. Had he been struck by a car?

"Four days ago, David said he didn't feel well. I let him stay home from school and rest, but when I came home in the middle of the afternoon, he was no better. I spent some extra money to buy part of a chicken and I made him some broth. He drank it all and went back to sleep, but the next morning, he looked worse. He was pale, and feverish, and he could keep no food in his belly. It all came out, one way or another."

"I let him stay home one more day, but that afternoon I saw that he was passing blood as well as the thin water of his bowels. He was so weak he couldn't eat, even when I brought the cup or spoon to his lips."

"When his father came home, we carried him to the hospital in a cart. That was two days ago." David's mother began crying again, so her daughter continued to explain.

"They asked my parents for money as soon as they got to the hospital, but they had none. Mother told them she would be getting paid by your father's clerk next week, but they said they could not even look at David without a hundred dollars up front. She begged and Father pleaded, and finally a doctor came out of the hospital and looked at David in the cart. He shook his head, and told my parents that David needed to be admitted to the hospital right away because the sickness was draining away his life force. He said David would need, not only medicines, but blood transfusions because his blood was leaving his body through his bowels. The doctor told them that it would probably cost a lot more money than we had. So they brought David back home."

"Where is the cart?" I asked.

"Behind the house," Adella waved her hand toward the rear door.

"Can you help with David? " I said, and when she nodded, I told her to wrap him in a warm blanket, and I would help her carry him out to the cart.

When we had done this, David's mother was standing by the cart, telling me that I didn't understand. "Yes, I do understand," I said, "It's a matter of money, and I am the son of a chief. They will let him into the hospital and they will take care of him if I say so."

It took almost an hour for the three of us to haul David to the hospital in the cart, and once, again, as we got to the emergency room entrance, the attendants waved us back, telling us that we needed money up front to bring in a new patient. I pushed past Adella and her mother and walked right up to the attendant in the best uniform. He was most

119

likely to be the one in charge.

"I am Antoni Bazia," I announced. "Henry Bazia is my father and I authorize, in his name, the treatment of this boy."

The attendant stared at me and then nodded. "I recognize you," he said. "You are the second son, the one who came to church last year in different clothes."

"Yes," I said, "that was me. Please bring this sick boy into the hospital. He needs help immediately!" I spoke with all of the authority I could muster, and it worked. The other two attendants lifted David carefully from the cart and laid him on a stretcher. Then they carried him quickly into the emergency room.

Adella and her mother tried to follow them, but the attendant in charge barred the way. "Please go home," he said. "Your son," he raised his eyebrows questioningly and I supplied the name David , "David will be cared for. Please come back tomorrow and talk to the doctors. You can see him then."

Then he turned to me, "I need your signature, Young Bazia,". He held out a clipboard with a very official looking document on it and handed me a pen. I wrote my father's name on the line. It looked like his real signature, but then, I had practiced the Bazia part many times.

I walked home with Adella and her mother, alternately dragging or pushing the cart. They must have thanked me a hundred times, but I urged them to save their gratitude until we knew that David would be okay.

The next day I ran home from school, an act which amazed

my three siblings who fully expected me to make my leisurely stroll home behind them as I always did, but I couldn't wait to go next door and find out how David was. I didn't even stop to shower and change my clothes. I just dashed to their house and pounded on the front door, but when no one opened it right away, I walked right in.

Adella was in the kitchen by herself. "My mother is at the hospital with the rest of the family," she said. "We can go there, too, if you would like."

"Do you know if he is better?" My heart was pounding in my chest. I could barely control my emotions, so deep was my concern for the life of this child.

"Yes," said Adella. "Our father went to the hospital last night and they told him that David was already much better. " She smiled shyly at me. "We cannot thank you enough, Toni." And then she kissed me on the lips.

For a moment we stood and stared at each other in the little kitchen, and then I said, "Let's go see him, Adella," and I opened the back door for her. Her gratitude embarrassed me and I wondered what she meant by the kiss. I had not helped them with the hope of any reward; it was only because they were my friends and the boy David was dying.

Adella had to walk fast to keep up with me, but I didn't want any more opportunities for her to say thank you, with or without kisses, and we got to the hospital very quickly. At the main desk, she asked for the room number for her brother and I followed her up the stairs.
Her mother was sitting in the hall with her husband and one of the middle daughters, Patricia. The other daughters were probably in the room with David, so Adella and I went

in.

I recognized the two youngest girls who were sitting on either side of David's bed. They immediately rose and pointed to the sign on the wall; ONLY TWO GUESTS PER PATIENT it read. I saw that there were three other beds in the long skinny room. David's was closest to the door.

As Miriam and Constance walked out into the hall to make room for their sister and me, they smiled and said, "Thank you, Toni!" I nodded and once again felt that flush of embarrassment and pleasure. I looked at David as Adella went and sat on the other side of the bed. He looked back at me and then he, too, smiled. It was a little smile and a weak smile, but it was a smile. It made me very happy to see it.

David came home from the hospital three days later; by the end of the following week, he was out in front of the house playing ball in the street. He always waved to me and sometimes I stopped and tossed the ball back and forth with him, but I decided that until this family had completely recovered from their intense gratitude to me, I should not visit often. I made it a point to go there when both the mother and father were home, and they always welcomed me in, but Adella and I never exchanged another kiss. It wasn't that I didn't like her; I just knew that to take advantage of her feelings would be very wrong and that it would reduce the joy I felt in helping to save David's life.

A month later, my Daddy called me into his office when I came home from school. He told me to close the door behind me when I entered, so I did as he asked and then I sat down in the chair opposite his desk. He handed me an official document, one which I immediately recognized. It had my rendition of my Daddy's signature on the bottom

122

line. It was now attached to a second official document which I examined carefully. At the bottom of this second page, I saw the numbers, $2500. This was David's hospital bill and that was a lot of money back then, even for my Daddy.

"This is not my signature," said my Daddy. "It looks like my signature, but it is not my signature."

"No, Daddy, " I said, "that is my writing of your name."

Daddy leaned back in his chair. "Why don't you tell me how this happened," he asked, and so I told him about the family, the mother of whom he already knew as she had been working for us for many years, the father who worked very hard in the market, and the four daughters and their precious young son who couldn't be admitted to the hospital even though he was dying because they didn't have any money.

"I would have taken care of this if they had asked me, " said my Daddy.

"They didn't know that this was something they should bring to their chief. They are very humble people," I explained.

"You should NOT have forged my signature," Daddy said.

"Will I be punished?" I asked, as I prepared an argument that my brothers and sister were in no way responsible for this crime of mine nor would they ever have thought of forging Daddy's name to anything.

"No," said my Daddy, as if he had read my thoughts. "If this kind of problem arises again, find me or find your mother. We will handle it."

"I was afraid to waste any more time. The boy was very ill."

"We will handle something like this next time. And we will not discuss this again."

And we never did. But sometimes when I am alone and thinking about that time in my life, the year I was first nine and then became ten on Christmas Day, I think about God's purpose and about how so many things that happened that year all contributed to saving the life of a little boy. It was a chain of events that puzzled and amazed me, beginning with my choice to dress differently from the rest of my siblings on a particular Sunday so that an attendant from the local hospital had cause to notice and remember me to the experiment of sending me to a bush village for three months where I learned the joys and responsibility of having a chief's influence on an entire family. David's life was a result of all of these events, and I could see God's purpose even more clearly in my life.

Chapter Twelve: Everything Changes

When I referred to much of my tenth year as uneventful, I was speaking in ignorance, because while I was going to school, taking my showers, wearing unique outfits, and talking with my father and the other powerful leaders of our country who frequently visited our home, something was happening between my mother and my father which would have an effect on all our lives. All four of us children were unaware of these events, although Ireni would later claim that she had a "funny feeling" that our parents were not as happy together as they had always seemed to us, but Ireni has often claimed to be more knowledgeable about people and the complexity of their relationships than her brothers. Perhaps being female, she is, but I would believe in her insights more strongly if I had been told about them beforehand rather than afterwards.

The end of my parents' marriage became public knowledge about one week after my eleventh birthday. It was the final Saturday of the Christmas holiday vacation, and I was enjoying my last two days of leisure by lying on my bed in complete idleness when a maid came to my door and said my mother wanted to see me. I was already dressed, so I jumped up, put on my shoes, and trotted down the hall to my mother's room. I might mention here that I didn't go to my mother's bedroom very often, and that, unlike the customs in much of the Western world of married people, this room was where my mother slept alone.

Separate sleeping quarters for husbands and wives are the custom in most upper class African families, especially in the family of the chief. It is believed that if a couple were to share a bedroom and sleep together all night in the same bed, this would make the man weak, and being a very traditional leader, my father followed this custom. My father had his own bedroom at some distance from my mother's, almost on the other side of the house, but this was not a new development or a sign of a rift in their marriage; it was the custom they had followed from the day they were wed.

My mother's bedroom was painted a pale green; her bed, large enough for two to sleep in if such a thing had been the custom, was covered with a pale green quilted satin spread. Many soft silky pillows, some white and others green, were arranged in front of the headboard. Her furniture was mahogany and extremely heavy. It was an elegant room and suited her personality perfectly. When I got there, she was sitting by the bed on a small boudoir chair which was also covered in pale green satin. She was stitching a button onto a blouse. It was typical of her to mend her own clothes even though we had enough servants that she need never lift a finger.

"Please sit, Toni," she said, and she gestured toward the bed. "I have something to tell you." I sat down carefully on the silky spread and waited.

"Your father and I have decided to divorce," she said. "And I am planning to move to Nzara. Your brothers and Ireni will be coming with me." She put a few more stitches into the button, and then broke the thread. "I would like you to come with us, even though you and I have not always been as connected to each other as I would have liked. I know that leaving your father will be very difficult for you, more so for you than any other of our children." Her voice caught a little on the word *our*, and suddenly I understood that as shocking and surprising as this change in the life of our family was to me, it was not something with which my mother was pleased.

I looked at her for several minutes. She said nothing more and looked back at me.
Finally I said what I knew might hurt her, but what was my most honest feeling. "I cannot leave my Daddy," I said. "He would be all alone."

My mother smiled a funny little smile and looked away from me. "He won't be alone," she said. "He has already been looking at another woman to marry. Do not make your choice based on what you believe he needs. Make it on what you need."

"But I want to be with my Daddy," I said. "I know you are

my mother, but..." At this point I had no words to explain how I felt, but my mother needed no explanation.

"I know you are more connected to your Daddy than to me," she said, "and I am not angry or offended. But, please remember, Toni, if you change your mind at some time, you can join me and live with your brothers and your sister."

"This new wife," I said, and then I hesitated because for only a second, terrible pain flashed across my mother's face, and I understood that she had not wanted her marriage to end. Just what had happened between them I would never really know, and besides, knowing would change nothing, at least as far as I and my brothers and sister were concerned. But it would help for me to know more about this woman who would be my stepmother, so, a little ruthlessly, I continued my question, "Does she have children?"

"She has four," my mother said, " and she is young enough to have more. You will have three stepsisters and one stepbrother although I doubt you will know him very well as he is older and attending university in Khartoum. Her daughters are still at home, however."

"Will we stay in this house?" I asked.

"That is the plan so far as I know," my mother said, "but your father will explain more to you this evening. I have already ordered that all my things and those of your brothers and sisters be packed as I plan to leave with them tomorrow. I want them to start school in Nzara on Monday, the same as everyone else." She spread out the blouse she had been fixing loosely on the bedspread beside me, and then she stood up and folded it neatly. She put it on the large stack of similar blouses on her dresser, a pile which I had not noticed when I entered her room.

I felt very strange as I watched her move around her room, opening drawers and removing items to add to the stack. I saw that her jewelry box was already gone from the dresser top, along with her ivory-handled brush, comb, and mirror set. More than once we had all been punished with the bricks because Ireni had stolen into my mother's bedroom and played with the jewelry or brushed her own hair with Mother's brush. I wondered if Mother would punish her children with the bricks in their new home, or would she adopt another set of rules? Perhaps in time there would be a new husband and Batista and Ireni would have to follow his discipline? Young Bazia was too old to be punished. Would they still call him young Bazia? After all, with my Daddy miles away in Khartoum, there could be no confusion. There would be only one Bazia in each family.

I turned around and left my mother's bedroom, still feeling like the earth had tilted on its axis and that although I had made the right choice for me, and I would continue to be able to be as close to my Daddy as I had always been, my life was permanently changed. No more watching my brothers and sister go by emotion. No more lining up in church in our uniforms. No more hearing my mother say, "Toni, you are not my child." Was this a change for the better? I couldn't say yet, but what I seemed to be losing were events that were familiar but not necessarily ones that I enjoyed. What wouldn't change, I thought, was my connection to my Daddy, the house I lived in, the servants who knew my little quirks and habits, and the close proximity to my Grandpop in the village although I had foreseen a time when he would not be there anymore. Someday in the not too distant future, he would sit down on the step by his front door, fall asleep in the warm afternoon sun, and not wake up for supper.

That night, after our own supper, a very quiet meal with only two diners, my Daddy and me, Daddy waved me into his office. "I understand your mother has told you we will separate," he began as he sat down behind his big desk. I nodded, and he continued, "She has also said that you would prefer to stay here with me?"

Again, I nodded and my Daddy smiled. "I am pleased that you feel our connection so strongly, Toni," he said, "but you must not make your decision based on a fear that I will be alone. I will be..."

And then for the first time in my life, I interrupted my Daddy, "I know; Mother told me you plan to marry again, but I want to be with you. You and I understand each other, and your father, my Grandpop, understands us both. I cannot imagine living away from either of you."

"All right," said my Daddy, and then he changed the subject, telling me about a new piece of legislation that the government had introduced the day before. I listened to him, but my thoughts were still flitting around in my head like bats. Who was this new wife? What would she be like? What would she feel toward the one child from my Daddy's first marriage who refused to leave and go with his mother? If she loved my Daddy, she should understand my choice, that I also loved him and couldn't go away. I thought about that some more; it made sense. Perhaps she and I would become friends. After all, we both loved my Daddy.

There was a great deal of commotion the following morning; all of the servants kept rushing in and out of the house, carrying boxes and suitcases and trunks of stuff belonging to my mother, my brothers, and my sister to the cars. At one point, Batista pointed out the window at the three cars in front of the house, all bearing piles of well-secured luggage on their roof racks and filled to bursting in the back seats. My mother and Ireni would ride up front with the driver in the first car, and my two brothers would ride in the front of the second. My brother Bazia kept asking the chauffeur if he could drive, but the servant only laughed and shook his head no.

My father stayed in his office where each of my siblings, in turn, went to say goodbye. There was no public parting between him and my mother; apparently they had already said their goodbyes, possibly weeks before this day. Thinking back, I could actually recall a day in October when two men in suits with briefcases had come to our house and gone into my father's office where my mother was also waiting. I nodded to myself. At the time, I hadn't understood what was happening, but now I did. I felt older and wiser, but also a little sad. There was nothing I could do to stop this change. I had to see this as something done, the glass of water dropped upon the floor, the water spilled, the glass broken, not fixable. There was no point in looking back. Our life as a family together was over.

I stepped out of the house and walked down toward the three vehicles. Two of them would return after the belongings were unloaded, but the first, a Lincoln which my mother had always used when she went out to shop or visit her friends, would stay at her new home. It was hers. As I stood by the front passenger door of this car, my mother got out again, and we hugged each other a little stiffly. Ireni smiled and waved but stayed in the front seat next to the driver. Then my mother got back in, and they drove away.

130

I walked back to the second car; Batista was also in the middle of the front seat, next to the driver, and like Ireni, he smiled and waved. My brother Bazia had, of course, commandeered the window seat, and he stuck his hand out for me to shake. "You have a cold heart, Toni," he said. "You don't seem to know how to feel things like the rest of us. I will not miss you very much." He looked straight ahead, and then the chauffeur put the car in gear and drove away.

As the third car drove by, the driver waved and called, "See you later, Toni," and I smiled and waved back. It was Sunday, but it didn't feel like Sunday because we weren't lining up to go to church. There was no church for my Daddy and me that day, perhaps because he didn't want to hear the whispers of shock and dismay as members of the tribe who had not yet heard about the separation speculated upon what it meant that only Henry Bazia and his second son Toni were sitting in the family pew.

Perhaps when my stepmother came to live here, we would start going to church again with her children, or maybe we would attend another church. Perhaps...I tried to turn my mind away from speculating about the unknowns in my future. It would be very unwise to waste my time and energy worrying about things that might never happen, so I walked back in the house and spent an hour looking over my clothes. Although I wore a uniform when I went to the village school, I had already developed the habit of changing into a nice shirt, tie, and dress pants after I got home and showered. That way when my Daddy came home from his city office and the important political leaders arrived after supper, I was ready.

As I examined my clothes, I made a list of new items I

would soon need, wrote down my sizes, and my color preferences, and then I found our shoppers in the kitchen and gave them the list. After that, I ate dinner with my Daddy. I read the Sunday newspapers in the living room. I showered again and changed in case we had evening guests. I spent the rest of that Sunday doing exactly what I would have done as if nothing had changed in my life.

Now you who are reading this will be convinced that I have a cold heart , just as my older brother said before he was driven away, but again, let me remind you that this book is about my philosophy, the way I have decided to live my life, and it is my purpose in writing this to explain my habits of thought, living, and decision-making to you. So I need to talk here about habits of living.

Human beings are creatures of habit; we eat at certain times, sleep at certain times, work and play and talk and, well, I don't need to list here all the different things we people do, but I would like to point out to you that our habits are very important to us, so much so that when they are altered, for example, we become confused and upset.

Many years after this twelfth year of my life, I had to take a job that required me to rise from my bed shortly after midnight and start work at one o'clock in the morning. I would finish my work shift just around sunrise, between seven and eight am. I was delivering newspapers from house to house in my car all over a large American city, Portland, Maine. It was not a job I especially enjoyed because it meant that I was awake and moving around the city in the dark while most other people were sleeping in their beds. It was lonely and boring, but I needed an income and at the time, jobs were very hard to get, so I did not complain. I focused on getting the papers delivered as efficiently as possible, and I used the time alone to think of

132

new ways to promote the causes of African refugees in the United States through my non-profit, Project Bazia. I made the best of this activity, but the hardest thing about it was the extreme change in my daily habits up to that point.

Before I began delivering newspapers at night so people could read the morning edition with their breakfast coffee, I lived just like most other people. I got up around eight am, showered, dressed, ate my breakfast, and then went off to do whatever my day as a non-profit director demanded such as attending meetings at the local juvenile detention center, visiting families in the South Sudanese diaspora community who needed my encouragement and support, or talking with my volunteers about what endeavors we were going to tackle next.

But now, I started my day eight hours earlier! The adjustment was very difficult; I had to struggle to stay awake as I drove through the dark streets of my route, but then, as the sun came up and I delivered the last few papers, I found that my old body clock was still ticking. Now my body was fully awake, and I wanted to continue my day just as I was accustomed to. I was faced with a very difficult challenge: my project needed my efforts to keep it going, but I also needed to work and earn money. How could I meet both challenges?

I created a very unique schedule of going back to bed for a few hours in the morning after I finished my route, then working on my project from eleven am until early evening, and finally grabbing as many hours of sleep as I could before rising in the dark again, but it was very difficult. My body was used to sleeping at least six hours straight; it was a very important habit. I found myself often becoming irritable about little things that normally wouldn't have bothered me at all. This was because my routine was disturbed, and I must admit that when I found another way to earn money, one that fit into a more normal schedule for me, I felt less stressed.

Now why am I wandering off into a story of working and struggling many years later, you are asking? I am trying to make it simple for you: I began by talking about habits, and sleeping is an important habit, one which is very difficult to change, but what I want you to think about is how important habits are to our physical, emotional, and mental well-being. If we had no habits, if our daily routine changed from moment to moment, it would create terrible stress upon our bodies, our minds, and our hearts. And often, when changes in our lives occur which are beyond our control, such as this great change in my family, whatever old habits we can still occupy ourselves with will reduce that stress a great deal. Habits are a source of comfort.

Now when we are children, our parents, if they are wise, will have a regular routine which the family follows. Meals should be at regular times, getting up in the morning should be about the same time every day, and bedtime should be fixed, although that can change a little at a time as a child gets older. Knowing what to expect and what to do throughout the day makes children feel safe. I am not saying the routine shouldn't ever change; in my Daddy's house, we were allowed to sleep later on the weekends and also stay up later at night, but this was also another part of the routine.

As I grew up under my Daddy's umbrella, I followed the family routine most of the time, but there were also habits I developed which were uniquely my own. I am betting you can guess that some of them involved taking showers and changing my clothes several times each day. As a

134

grown man, I still follow that routine because I know it contributes to my sense of well-being. I watch television and listen to the radio for the daily news many times throughout the day, not only because I am interested in what is happening all over the world, but because it is my habit. Again, if I cannot follow my routine, even if there is nothing going wrong in the rest of my life, I become unbalanced.

So here is my recommendation to you, whatever your age. Think about your daily routine. You could write it down on a piece of paper like this, "I get up at ..., I eat breakfast at...., I leave the house at ...". I think you get the idea. Make sure you include the parts of your routine that are truly your own, that you look forward to doing every day. If you don't have any, create one or two and then put this into your day until this, too, has become a habit. Listening to music that you really like is a good habit to establish, or reading, if only for an hour. Some people find that regular physical exercise, even a brisk walk around the block every day after lunch, keeps them calm and relaxed. The important thing is doing some things the same way and at the same time every day.

Now I am not trying to turn you into a robot whose entire day is filled with the same actions over and over again! Your regular habits of sleep, meals, and school will automatically create some routine, but the important thing is to have habits that are uniquely yours. And this is why. When things get tough, and you find yourself getting upset about events which you cannot change, follow your routine just as if nothing unusual has happened. This will take your mind off your troubles. It will help you think more clearly and make you feel like you have some control over the world around you. Your routine will keep you moving on, moment by moment, and this will help you overcome

135

the challenges in your life which are bound to come.

Chapter Thirteen: Changes and Challenges

Several weeks passed during which the most significant changes in our home were an increase in space and a decrease in noise. The departure of my three siblings and my mother meant that there were now four empty bedrooms. Ireni's departure meant a considerable reduction in laundry, and my mother's absence (because she always demanded elaborate sauces and stews) a more relaxed menu at mealtime. My Daddy and I had always preferred very simple foods, meats well cooked, sweet potatoes, occasional mixes of spiced rice, and fresh vegetables so the cook's job was much easier. The maids had such a light workload that they almost burst into song. Without my brothers, there was very little dirt and debris tracked inside as both my Daddy and I were very neat people and always wiped our shoes on the mat before we came through the door.

Many of my father's political cronies would drop by right after the evening meal, and we would all sit in the living room and talk until very late at night. This was probably the period in my life when I learned to get by with less than eight hours of sleep, but I also discovered that without the presence of Ireni and Batista who couldn't seem to move around the house without talking, yelling, or slamming doors, it was so quiet when I came home from school that I could take a long nap to refresh myself before the exciting evening started.

But one day, the tranquility of life alone with my Daddy came to an end. It was on a Friday. I had come home from school and was headed toward my room, already taking off

136

my school uniform shirt so I could take a quick shower before I threw myself onto my bed and fall into a deep sleep. I was so engrossed in my own thoughts that I failed to see that there were four strangers sitting in the living room. They were all small, they were all female, and upon close examination, they all looked very much alike.

The one I thought to be the eldest was seated on a club chair right next to the sofa. She was wearing a white linen suit, and she had a vibrant orange head wrap tied over her hair. Corners of the elaborate headwrap stuck out on one side at a jaunty angle. She had golden earrings on her earlobes, each one as big as a wrist bangle. Her eyes were heavily lined with kohl and her lashes coated with thick mascara. She had especially full lips which she had painted with coral lipstick. She was attractive, but in a very obvious way. "You must be Toni," she said. She smiled, revealing very large, very white, teeth. "Do you always begin to undress in the living room? Now, now, now, we shall have to train you to do otherwise, especially since there will be three young ladies living here with you."

The woman rose from the chair as I fumbled back into my uniform shirt. She put her right hand out, so I shoved my arm through the right sleeve of my shirt and took it. I bowed slightly as I shook her hand, and she smiled again her very toothy grin. "Well," she said, "at least you have some manners. My name is Mary, and I am going to be your stepmother. You can call me..." she hesitated for a moment, and then finished her directive, "Mary."

I bowed slightly again. "Welcome to our home, Mary," I said. Then I looked curiously at the three young ladies on the couch. They too were wearing white linen suits and bright headwraps, one purple, one yellow, and one pink.

137

Mary let go of my hand and gestured at each girl in turn, "These are my daughters, Lydia, Lucia and Letitia. My son Osborn is away at the university, but I am sure you will be meeting him soon."

Again I smiled politely. Then I shook hands with each girl and welcomed her to our home as I had done with their mother. They didn't smile or say anything; they held my hand for only a moment. They stared at me and then as if they were joined at the hip, they turned toward their mother. "Is this boy going to be sleeping in the same part of the house as us? We don't think that will be good." said Lydia, the tallest and probably the oldest daughter.

"Yes, Mama," said Lucia, "I agree with Lydia. I don't think he should be in a room near us. He probably makes a lot of noise." Lucia scrunched up her nose like a noise was also a bad smell.

"I think that his room is the second one on the right," said Letitia. "I think I would like that room. He can move somewhere else in the house."

"I shall speak to Henry," said Mary. "I am sure he will agree." She stared at me for a moment. "But perhaps Toni is enough of a gentleman that we won't even have to bother his father with this request. What do you say, Toni? Can your new sister Letitia take your room? I know that there are empty rooms in the wing where your father sleeps. I am sure you would prefer to be near him anyway. Then you can make as much noise as you like."

"I am a very quiet person, " I said, "but it's okay. I will speak to the maids and they can put my things in the room next to my Daddy's."

There was a sound of giggling, and then one of the girls, I think it was Lucia, mumbled, "He calls his father Daddy. Just like a little boy."

Thus began the period of my life where my ability to not go by emotion was severely tested. This new family of women that now outnumbered my Daddy and me two to one seemed to delight in finding fault or mocking anyone who crossed their path, with one exception. They were never rude to my Daddy, and they made sure that he never saw them making fun of me or the servants. Three servants quit two weeks later, but I didn't find the girls' constant teasing or criticism especially painful, mostly because I didn't agree with what they said. My words and my behaviors had always been carefully considered and planned so that they fit with what I thought was correct and appropriate; there was no self-doubt to undermine my self-respect which meant they could attack me anyway they wanted to, but it meant no more than having a large and annoying fly buzzing around my head. But there were four flies and they were relentless and annoying.

At first I found myself avoiding areas of the house where the four of them might gather during the day, but when I realized that I was allowing them to control me, however slightly, I changed my behavior and made it a point to appear in the dining room when they ate breakfast as well as joining them in the living room for an hour every afternoon when I returned from school. While they asked silly questions and then ridiculed my polite answers, I continued to smile and say, "That's okay." or "Do you think so?"

The girls were too unintelligent to understand that my tolerance made them look foolish, but their mother was more perceptive. Very soon she stopped speaking to me unless it was absolutely necessary. She smiled politely at me, using that special smile which never leaves the lips to go to the eyes. Occasionally I caught a little gleam in her eyes as I nodded at one of her daughters and said, "That's okay." She was studying me.

Fortunately for me, because my father was not yet officially married to Mary, she was not able to intrude upon the wonderful evenings with the important men who visited us almost every day. I was convinced that this would not change after my father married her because even my very dignified and highly educated mother had not joined us for our political discussions very often, although when she did, her observations were always highly regarded. I remember one leader remarking that it was very pleasant to get "the lady's point of view" on an issue, but I greatly doubted that Mary would be encouraged to join us in the living room to offer hers. I don't think she would have understood much of what we talked about anyway. She was, to say it the kindest way I know, a traditional woman, interested in new clothes, sharing local gossip with other women, and making sure that everyone knew how important she was as the wife of the tribal chief.

I did not fault her for this; my mother had been unusually well-informed about politics for a woman of her generation because of her family background, but Mary came from a lower class family where a woman's education was not considered necessary. The truth of this was apparent when I learned that all three of her daughters were planning on being done with school when they completed grade twelve; even that minimal education was unimportant to them. A few days after they moved in, Mary enrolled them in the same school that I attended. And that set in motion the next cause for their resentment of me.

At the end of the first week of their attendance at my school, my Daddy entered the dining room for supper and made the following request. "I would like to see some your schoolwork," he said, addressing his three new stepdaughters. The girls stared blankly back at him as if he had spoken in an unfamiliar language, so he repeated his request. This time it sounded more like a command.

They looked at their mother for her consent, and she made a little motion with both her hands, like "shoo, shoo, shoo", so they scurried off. In a few moments, they returned, each girl with a couple of papers in her hands. They handed them to my Daddy who sat down in his chair at the head of the table.

He studied them carefully, wagging his head from side to side in disapproval. "This will not do," he said. "This is not good." He handed the papers back to the girls and continued, "When I pay for someone's education, whether the student is a member of my tribe, or one of my own children, I expect that student to do very good, if not excellent, work. There was no paper there that even received a grade of acceptable, let alone good! You will all have to improve or there will be consequences."

I knew what the consequences would be: the bricks. I was wondering if Mary had been told how her children would be disciplined, when suddenly my stepmother spoke up. "What about Toni?" she asked. Her usually sweet voice was almost a whine, but she got it under control almost immediately.

"Toni knows what I expect," said my Daddy, " but if you want me to inspect his papers..." He pointed toward the door. "Toni?"

141

I raced out of the room and dashed to my bedroom. I gathered up a big stack of recently returned tests and homework, along with an essay I had written on the present system of government in Khartoum. I knew I was about to win this battle: every single paper was at least an A, and several had A+!

When I brought them back to the dining room, my father spread them across the table. "Now this is what I expect from one of my children," he said. I smiled and looked across the table at my three stepsisters. They were not smiling. They were not happy. They were jealous of my Daddy's praise and of my success. And, they hated me more than ever.

Mary spoke up in their defense, saying that the school they had attended before was not staffed with good teachers, but my Daddy wasn't going to accept that excuse. "If you need to hire tutors for them, to help them catch up," he said, "by all means, hire tutors.
But you also need to explain to your children that I expect them to do well in school. You need to tell them what happens when my expectations are not met."

Mary's face tightened around her eyes and mouth. I knew he had told her about the bricks.

The next day I noticed that my three stepsisters did not return home right after school. They had all stayed behind to talk with their teachers about how they could improve their grades. At the supper table that night, Mary told my Daddy about this, and he nodded his approval. Then she said that she was also looking for a prospective husband for the oldest girl, Lydia. She was only seventeen, but that was not too young to marry right after she graduated from high school. "My daughters are not interested in going to college," Mary said. "They are like me. They prefer to be wives and mothers." My Daddy didn't object to this. It would have been unreasonable to expect otherwise; they had not grown up under his umbrella.

After that,much of Mary's socializing every day was directed toward finding acceptable husbands for her daughters. At the dinner table, where she sat on my Daddy's left hand instead of at the other end of the table where my mother used to sit, she frequently discussed this with him, naming prospects and listening to his judgments very solemnly.

She was traditional in other ways. She changed her clothes and put on fresh makeup so that she looked her best as she greeted him when he came through the front door. She asked him how his day had gone. She would order refreshment for him if he wanted it. She was charming, feminine, even a little flirtatious, and my Daddy seemed to like it. Not that my own mother had allowed herself to look slovenly or treat my Daddy as if she didn't respect him, but she was not so attentive, often having matters of her own to deal with outside of the home, matters befitting the wife of the chief. Other than going shopping or having coffee with women like herself, Mary didn't leave our home. And Mary was at least ten years younger than my mother.

The next change in my life with my new family was so lacking in subtlety that I was in shock for several days. It began right after my Daddy announced at the supper table that he must travel to Juba the following morning and wouldn't return for a week. I watched as Mary's eyes watered and her lower lip trembled. She was a very good actress; Ireni could have taken lessons from her! As she held back her tears, my Daddy explained that he would return as soon as he could, and she nodded, putting on a brave little smile.

143

The following morning I saw her waving at him from the living room window as his chauffeur drove him away, and for a moment, I wondered if she actually did care about him, but as soon as his car was out of sight, she turned around, looked at me, and smiled the most genuine smile I had yet seen on her face. "Have a good day at school, Toni, " she said. This puzzled me because she had never said this to me before unless my Daddy was also in the room. She was definitely up to something. But what?

That afternoon when I returned from school, I found out. I was now almost twelve years old and growing very fast, so instead of showering and changing, or taking a nap, I always headed straight for the kitchen. The cook found this amusing, but she was usually waiting with a sandwich, or bread and soup, fruit and milk. Sometimes she fixed me eggs or cooked up some cold rice with a peppery sauce. I always ate whatever she made and still had plenty of room for my supper later in the evening.

But this day, the cook was not there. Mary was standing next to the refrigerator. She appeared to be waiting for me. "You must wait for supper, Toni, " she said when I helped myself to a glass from the cupboard. "I have been watching you eat and eat and eat since I arrived. You can only eat at mealtimes from now on." She took the glass from my hand. And I will supervise what and how much. It is my duty as your father's wife to do this." She waved her fingers at me like one would shoo away a chicken.

My stomach growled. She said nothing more and put the glass in the cupboard. I left the room.

That night at the supper table I ate everything that was put on my plate and asked for more, but although Letitia got a

144

second piece of steak, and Lucia got another portion of sweet potatoes, I only got one helping of each item served, and my single piece of steak was the smallest one of all. I reached for more rolls, but Mary deftly removed the breadbasket from my end of the table. I did manage to grab a second mango as the fruit bowl was passed around, but when I raised my glass of milk to my lips, I discovered that it was almost sour. I frowned and called for the maid to replace it, but Mary was watching. "If you don't like what is put in front of you, " she said, "you will have to go hungry." And then she smiled her nasty little smile.

And then, despite all of the discipline I could muster, despite the self-control I had practiced all of my life, I could not smile back and say, "It's okay." I knew what she was doing: she was hoping I would give up and leave, go live with my mother like my siblings. I knew she didn't like me at all and she didn't have to; I could live with that. But she didn't care about my Daddy either.

She just wanted to be a chief's wife with as much control as she could get. She was clever, I granted her that. After all, she had tried this second campaign to get rid of me while my Daddy was away. The cook was also having an unexpected day off as well as the maids, so there had been no witnesses earlier to our confrontation in the kitchen. She was going to be very difficult to defeat, but I believed then as I still do that life is about challenges, so I stared right back at her, rose from the table with my mango, and said, "I will see you at breakfast."

Because my Daddy was away, there were no visitors that night so I went to my new room in the other wing and threw myself on the bed. I was still hungry. I ate my mango.
I was still hungry. I thought about sneaking down to the

145

kitchen, but I was certain that Mary would have expected me to do this. I counted the money I had in my top desk drawer. It wasn't very much, but if before my Daddy came back, I could supplement my diet with a few items from a store, I wouldn't starve to death. In fact, if I reminded the shopkeeper who I was, he would probably put the charges on my Daddy's account. I felt a little better and was now able to fall asleep.

Breakfast was very similar to supper; no second helpings, small portions for me to begin with, and the milk was even more curdled. I noticed that my stepsisters were drinking their milk as if there was nothing wrong with theirs. There probably wasn't. I left the table early and stopped at a store on my way to school. I bought three rolls and a quart of milk, all of which I ate outside on the street.

This was the routine I would follow for the rest of the week, with the exception of Friday. After school on Friday, I stopped at the store and bought a dozen rolls, some meat pies, and several bottles of juice. I charged them to Henry Bazia and the store owner never said anything. Loaded down with my groceries, I was heading home when I saw my stepmother's car drive by. She was staring at me out of the window. This was not good.

I waited until her car disappeared, and then I took a shortcut back to the house, running as fast as I could. It wouldn't be very smart to hide the food in my room; that would be the first place she would look. The kitchen wouldn't be a good choice either; I hadn't seen our cook since my Daddy had gone away. She might have been visiting relatives, but it was also possible that Mary planned to replace her. One of the maids was new also. If this continued, there would be no one left in the house I could trust.

146

The shortcut home ended near the garage, and I breathed a sigh of relief. Mary had not yet returned, so I had time to hide my extra rations for the weekend.

The chauffeur that usually drove me around if I asked was polishing the old blue Chevy sedan. He smiled at me as I walked up. "I need to hide something in the garage, " I said. He looked puzzled so I continued, "It's some presents for my Daddy. You know he has been in Juba, and..." I hesitated, "I miss him."

I looked down as if such an emotion was unbecoming in a young man, but the chauffeur smiled. "You are a good son, Toni, " he said. "Why don't you hide your gifts in that cabinet? Nobody but me would ever go in there." He pointed to a small wooden closet in the corner of the car bay. I hurried over, stuffed in the bags of food, and went back outside just in time to see Mary's car come into the yard. I acted as if I were watching the chauffeur polish the car.

Mary got out when her driver opened the door, followed by her three daughters. She was carrying her purse and a large shopping bag. "I see, Toni, that you went shopping this afternoon too," she commented. "Where are your bags?"

"Me? Shopping? Bags?" I looked confused.

"Yes, I saw you with some shopping bags, on the street in town."

"Oh," I said, thinking fast, "I was carrying those for someone else, for an old lady."

"Don't lie to me, " Mary snapped. "There was no old lady with you."

"You couldn't see her, " I said. "She was on the other side of me. She was very short."

Mary stared at the chauffeur who was now buffing the hood as if his life depended upon its sheen. "Did Toni have any bags with him when he got home today?" she said.

"No," said the chauffeur, and he studied the hood of the car some more. "No bags, Missus."

Mary stared at both of us for a minute and then flung herself around and marched toward the house. She was obviously angry, but I knew she would not give up with her plan to drive me away. But she would not win. I would not go away.

The next two days seemed very long, but finally I saw my Daddy's car come into the yard. I raced outside to greet him. He looked very tired. How could I burden him with my complaints that his soon-to-be-new wife was abusing me? I decided I would wait for a few days. Perhaps if she saw that her plan had not worked, she would give up. After all, my Daddy didn't go away very often. Maybe...

But as soon as Mary came out of the house, I realized that my Daddy's homecoming would not be peaceful. Her face was once again set in a grim mask which quickly changed to the sad face with the trembling lips and tear-filled eyes. "Oh, Henry," she cried, "I am so glad you are back. And here is your son. I am sure he has been complaining about me to you already! I have had such a time with him!"

Chapter Fourteen: More Challenges

I listened politely as Mary proceeded to tell my Daddy the most amazing series of lies about my sins during his absence. According to her, I had complained constantly about everything in the house from my new room to the laundry to the sheets and blankets on my bed, but especially about the food. She said I was whining all the time. Everything was too salty or totally lacking in flavor! The meat was too rare or so overcooked as to be tough and inedible! The vegetables were undercooked or else they were mushy! And at almost every meal I had demanded a fresh glass of milk, claiming that the original glass was sour!

"Toni was so picky that the cook finally quit and went back to her native village," said Mary. "I have had to do some of the cooking myself because no one wants to work for us. Everyone in your house is miserable." At this point she spun around dramatically and pointed at me, "And it is all Toni's fault!"

"Is this true?" my Daddy said, looking at me.

"Not exactly," I answered, "but the milk in my glass was sour. The other milk, in their glasses," and I pointed to Lydia, Lucia, and Letitia, "was just fine."

"That's ridiculous," said Mary. "How could the same milk turn sour in a different glass?" Then she moved between my Daddy and me. "If you talk to the man who runs the village store, you are in for an even bigger surprise. Toni has been stopping there every day before and after school to buy bread or meat pies or quarts of milk. And he is charging this food to your account, Henry! Such a waste of your money when there is perfectly good food..."

"Enough!" said my Daddy. "Can't a man come home from a long trip and find peace? Toni, I don't know what has come over you to act this way! I really don't know what to think." And with that, my Daddy took his briefcase from the car and went into the house. Mary grinned in triumph at me, and then she told the driver to bring my Daddy's suitcase inside. I followed the man down the hall, went into my own bedroom, and closed the door.

I sat on my bed and stared into space for a long time. Then I cried like a little baby. My Daddy, who had known me all my life, who knew I always told the truth even when it meant I would be punished with the bricks, did not believe me. He believed her, this evil woman who had only one thought on her mind which was to drive me away. I didn't know what to do.

Just then there was a tap on my door. "Yes?" I said.

It was my stepmother. "Your father wants you to come to his office," she said.

"Thank you," I answered. I wiped the tears from my face and opened the door.

Mary was still standing there. She looked very happy. "Why don't you just give up?" she asked. "I am sure your mother will welcome you into her house. Your father doesn't need all of this conflict in his home. If you really care about him, you would understand that. So just give up, Toni!"

"I don't give up," I said. Then I walked away toward my Daddy's office.

Later that day I had to hold the bricks for the first time in more than a year; my Daddy had phoned the shopkeeper and when the man confirmed that I had been in there every day buying food and charging it to his account, he was convinced that Mary was telling the truth and that I was lying. Part of his doubt of me was based on the time two years before when I had taken the neighbor's boy to the hospital, to save his life, and charged medical treatments to my Daddy. That bill had been $2500, and my Daddy had warned me to never do that again. The shopkeeper's bill was less than twenty dollars, but, still, I had used my Daddy's name to pay for something, and that was forbidden.

I was a little puzzled when I went to room where the brick punishment was usually performed because at first there was nobody there but me. If we were following the normal rules of our family, my stepsisters should have been there also. Apparently Mary had even more power over my Daddy than I realized.

I knelt on the rug and stretched out my arms. Daddy put two bricks in each of my hands. "Thirty minutes," he said. Behind him, I saw Mary and her three daughters in the doorway.

"Do we have to, Mama?" asked Lydia.

"Yes," said my Daddy, " but you three have to hold only one brick in each hand for ten minutes. And then I will take the bricks away, but you must keep your arms out and watch Tony while he finishes his punishment. All three of you need to understand the discipline of this family, but because you are new, I will not insist on the same time."

The three girls knelt on the rug and stretched out their

151

arms. Daddy put the bricks in place and then stepped away. I was ashamed to admit that my arms had already begun to ache, it had been so long since I had done this, but I held my head high and stared into space, concentrating on my breathing and trying to relax my tense muscles. Many people think that tensing the muscles gives you more strength in them, but this isn't the case at all. Tension actually consumes more energy and creates pain.

I darted a quick glance at Letitia. The tendons in her neck were drawn tight and there were beads of sweat on her forehead. Lydia was holding up a little better, but she had closed her eyes and her breathing was speeding up. Lucia, who was kneeling at the end of the line, directly in front of where her mother stood in the doorway, was in the worst shape of all. She was sweating so much that her blouse was soaked and lines of pain furrowed her brow. I couldn't imagine how it felt to do this punishment for the first time when you were not used to any hard work at all. I remembered how much it hurt me before I went away on my summer vacation with the family in the village. I almost felt sorry for my stepsisters.

"I can't do this!" shrieked Lucia, and she dropped both bricks on the rug.

When she started to stand up, my Daddy came forward and pressed his hands on her shoulders. "You must, " he said. "And, because you gave up, you must start again, from the beginning. Put out your hands!" And then he put the bricks back.

My Daddy moved to the other girls and took their bricks away. "You see, Lucia, you were almost finished," he said, "but now you have ten minutes more."

152

"But, Henry," said Mary, "this isn't fair! My girls didn't do anything wrong!"

"Life is unfair," said my Daddy. "And if we raise our children to believe that it is, we are telling them the greatest lie of all. If they leave our umbrella and go out into the world thinking that life will be fair and they will always get whatever they want, they will get a really big surprise! And they won't be strong enough to handle this new and important truth. They will suffer a great deal and be very unhappy. Some don't survive."

Mary began to cry; she was one of the few women I have ever met who had perfected the art of crying and still looking pretty. She didn't scrunch up her eyes or furrow her brow. She only let her lower lip droop a little in a soft pout while the tears welled up and ran down her cheeks. But her skill this time had no effect. My Daddy turned his back and waited for the punishment times to end.

For the next six months, Mary didn't try any tricks because my Daddy didn't leave Khartoum for distant cities. Gradually my life returned to something like normal; I got the same food as my stepsisters, although it was never enough as I was still growing. I went to school and got excellent grades while Lydia, Lucia, and Letitia struggled to bring home "Acceptable" and "Good" work. They were not punished for this, which was a relief for me because I would have been punished, too, despite the fact that I had many "Perfect" marks. Maybe that was why my Daddy didn't discipline them, because in some way he knew it would hurt me, but for many weeks, he seemed to avoid me, and more than once, when I knocked on his office door, he said he was "too busy" to talk right then.

The important men came and went every night, and I was

153

still allowed to sit in on their discussions. This was some comfort to me, but my Daddy seemed very distant, almost cold, and this was hard to bear. It was one more challenge to face, one which made me realize that someday he would be cold in the ground and I would no longer be able to talk to him at all. I thought about that inevitable truth often while I struggled with my own pain. This is the nature of a challenge: it makes you appreciate the good things in your life more while at the same time it shows you that nothing lasts forever. And, of course, as my Daddy said, a challenge makes you stronger.

Then finally the moment I thought I had been waiting for arrived; late one afternoon, my Daddy sent one of the maids to ask me to come to his office. I was just finished with a shower and had selected a nice outfit, but now it didn't look special enough for my first private talk with my Daddy in months, so I picked another shirt, this one pale lilac and then a different tie, one with very dignified charcoal grey and deep magenta diagonal stripes, and got dressed. I ran down the hall and knocked on his office door.

He told me to enter and I walked in and sat down in the chair opposite him. He was studying a piece of paper carefully, so I said nothing until he was done. Then he put the paper on his desk, and spoke, "I want your advice, Toni."

I was astounded by his request. After months of cold silence, he wanted my advice. It wasn't like he had never listened to my opinion before; he had, in fact, asked me what I thought about all kinds of issues and decisions over the years. He often said that I gave him a different perspective on everything and that he valued it greatly, but now, after such a long time without our talking, I felt like I could weep with joy.

I kept a serious expression on my face. "What is your concern? " I said.

"There is an opportunity for someone in the Sudanese military to go to the United States and study weaponry, particularly small arms and rifles. The education would take about one year after which the student would return to Sudan and be invaluable in the selection of armaments as well as the training of troops. He would gain great status, not only in rank, but in importance to the government."

"Have you been asked to do this?" I said.

"No," my Daddy went on, "there is a test. They have limited the number of candidates to two thousand, but only the two candidates who have the highest scores would be selected to go. What I want to know from you is, should I take the test?"

I thought for only a moment and then I said, "Of course you should take the test."

My Daddy nodded and smiled. "I thought you would say that. You don't believe in turning down any challenge, no matter how..."

I waved one hand to make him pause, "It is not only the challenge. I know you will have one of the two top scores. And you will go to the United States for one year to study."

"How do you know this?" My Daddy looked perplexed.
155

"I don't know how I know; I just know." And even as I rejoiced that my Daddy was going to travel to the most wonderful country in the world, maybe setting in motion the possibility of my going there myself someday, my heart sank because I knew this meant that he would leave for a whole year while I remained here in this house with Mary and her unpleasant daughters. I would face glasses of sour milk for a whole year.

And everything happened just as I had predicted: my Daddy took the test along with 1,999 other people, and he got the top score! Then, because the program about weaponry began in less than a month, our house was the focus of much shopping and packing so that he would have appropriate clothing to wear in America. I was happy that my prediction had come true because I knew how much this would improve my Daddy's status with the Khartoum government. As an African, and a Christian at that, he had not been looked at for promotions like Moslems of Arabic descent. If he achieved higher rank and was perceived as knowledgeable about weaponry, he might also be listened to with more respect when he spoke about improving the condition of Sudanese people who lived in the south.

But of course, for me, things would not improve. In fact, they would probably get worse, for, without the presence of my Daddy, Mary could pursue her long term goal of forcing me to leave my home. By now, most of the servants I had known for many years had been replaced with people loyal to her. Only our shoppers were still with us, but they spent most of their time out of the house fetching things desired by Mary and her three spoiled daughters, and since they lived in constant fear of being fired, they wouldn't have helped me anyway.

156

The family that I had befriended years before still lived in the house next door, so I had at least one refuge I could turn to for a moment of peace and perhaps a little friendly social life. My Daddy had ordered his accountant to give me a generous monthly allowance; I could use this to make sure I didn't starve to death. I would be in school for most of the weekdays, and it would also be possible for me to travel to visit friends and relatives in other cities during vacations. So, I decided that I would stay there in that house. I would obey Mary's orders; I would not lose my temper with her or with my stepsisters; in short, I would not give up. She would not win.

Now at this point many of you are probably wondering why I would do this. Yes, yes, we know life is full of challenges, but what is the point of facing a challenge when you don't have to? Why not take the easy road? In my case, why not contact my mother and go live with her, Ireni, and Batista?

The answer lies in the advice I gave to Batista so long ago when he asked me how to handle the boys who mocked him on the streets of Khartoum. Do you remember?

I told him not to fight, but I also told him not to run away. I told him to face the challenge of their hurtful words with dignity and politeness. I told him that he must be an example to them of proper behavior. If you remember these instructions, then you may also remember why. Once you start to back down and run away from the challenges of your life, you begin a journey down a long and terrible road of self-defeat. You will not only be letting the challenges win; you will be helping them! It is one of the most important beliefs in my philosophy. You must never give up. Even if the challenge overwhelms you and somehow destroys you, you must not give up. When you

157

give up, you become your own worst enemy.

Many years later I was working at the American Embassy in Gabon. I did a lot of different things, including caring for all of the automobiles in the large garage next to the Embassy, driving diplomats to and from appointments while also protecting them, or acting as a security guard for social functions. And because by this time I was totally fluent in Arabic, in the evenings I went to gathering places frequented by the Arabs who lived in this city. I dressed like an Arab and I socialized like an Arab. And I reported any information I heard in these places to the Embassy because even at this time, there was great fear in many nations of the activity of Arab terrorists. As a result of my various responsibilities and because I lived at the Embassy, I had diplomatic immunity.

One day I was leaving an elegant hotel in the city. I had just dropped off some papers to a visitor from the United Kingdom who was staying there. I left the elevator, crossed the lobby, nodded to the desk clerk with whom I often chatted, and walked toward the door. There was a tall woman who was coming toward me across the lobby and, as it happened, we both chose the same path around the furniture, a path which brought us face to face. We both stopped moving.

"Move aside," she said with a little wave of her hand. She was evidently a woman with complete belief in her own importance. In fact, I expect she thought she was the center of the universe.

I stared at her for a moment without moving, and then, without any tone of malice or sarcasm, I replied, "Why don't *you* move aside?"

She reared back in shock. "Why should I move?" she demanded.

I smiled, "Why should I?"

"You should move, " she said, her nostrils flaring in anger, "you should move because you are nobody and I am somebody."

"Everybody is important, " I replied. And I didn't move out of her way.

She gave a little snort of breath, expressing both her frustration and her disbelief in my words. Then she raised both her hands and pushed me in the chest. She pushed me pretty hard.

I reeled a little, but I still didn't move. "I don't think you want to do that again," I said. "It would not be wise."

She looked me up and down and then she raised her left hand and snapped her fingers, calling with this sound to a bellhop who was standing next to the desk."Boy," she said to the bellhop, "go get me a policeman."

The bellhop scurried out the door onto the street. While we waited, the lady and I stared at each other. She was obviously getting more and more angry, but I remained calm and just smiled. This was going to be very interesting.

In less than ten minutes, the bellhop returned with two policemen. The lady waved to them to join us, and while she was explaining how rude I had been, they asked us both to show them our passports. I took mine out of my inside coat pocket where I always kept it and handed it to one officer who immediately noticed the large seal just inside the cover which proclaimed my diplomatic connection.

The lady fished around in the shiny snakeskin purse which dangled from her wrist, found her passport, and gave it to the other officer. He examined it, made a few notes in a small notebook he carried, and then handed it back to her. All this time the lady kept talking about how she wanted me to move. She proclaimed several times that she was not accustomed to being confronted by people as arrogant as I obviously was. She insisted that they should arrest me for assault.

The officer who had examined my passport tried to explain to her that under the circumstances, they couldn't charge me with assault, but that even if I had done something worse than simply refusing to move out of her way, I had diplomatic immunity; they couldn't arrest me for anything. Then he asked me for my side of the story.

"Yes," I said, "I did refuse to move even though this lady asked me to move several times. Then she tried to shove me out of the way."

"She touched you?" said the officer.

"Yes, I did," said the lady, not waiting for me to speak. "I put my hands on his chest and I pushed him as hard as I
160

could!" She looked at the officers and the small crowd of bystanders who had by now gathered to watch this little drama as if to say, "How about that!"

"You shouldn't have done that," said the second policeman. "You assaulted him!" Then he turned to me. "Do you want her arrested?"

The lady's eyes grew as large as saucers. She obviously had no idea what she had done or what she had started when she demanded that I move. I studied her for a moment, and then I said, "No, I will be happy with an apology."

The lady gulped. Then she frowned. She was still angry, but she certainly didn't want to take the chance that these policemen would indeed arrest her if she didn't, so she looked down at her feet and mumbled, "I'm sorry."

"I can't hear you, " I said.

"I'm sorry," she repeated as she looked me in the eye.

"Apology accepted, " I said, and then I watched her backtrack around the furniture and choose a completely different route across the lobby. I waited a few minutes and then started toward the door, following the two policemen who were waggling their eyebrows at each other. They couldn't wait to get out on the street and talk about this encounter.

Behind me, I heard the lady speak again, "Wait!" she said.

I turned around and stared at her.

"Wait, *please*," she said.

I walked back toward her, keeping my distance. I had no idea what she wanted, but as I have said, I do not give up and pull away from people, no matter how unpleasant they become.

"You are a very unusual man, " she said.

"I know," I said. "Would you like to have a cup of coffee? We could talk about this." She nodded, and we did indeed talk for at least an hour in a nearby coffee shop.

Now you are probably wondering why I did that. No, it was not because I found her attractive. It wasn't anything like that at all. What I saw when I looked at this lady was someone who needed to learn that she was not important as she seemed to think she was. I wanted her to learn that everybody is important, and that if we all treated the rest of humanity that way, the world would be a better place.

My Daddy returned from America at the end of that year and began enjoying the benefits of his higher status. Although I did go away to school in Cairo and other places from time to time, I continued to return to that house where I lived with Daddy, Mary, and the three stepsisters for about five years. Living there was always a challenge, and I never felt that I actually made much progress with Mary or the girls like I did with the woman in the hotel, but it was a very important experience for me. It made me stronger while it taught me at the same time that the

162

hardest thing in the world to do is to change other people.

Chapter 15: Full Circle

There is nothing more beautiful than a circle. Round, complete, united, whole, a circle makes perfect sense. The end flows into the beginning, and the beginning flows into the end.

Wheels, planets, our faces, all are circles. A circle has no corners to jab you or angles where mysterious things can hide. Circles are symmetrical in every direction. Take your first finger and curve it around to touch your thumb. What do you have? You have the sign OK. If you and your friends all join hands together, you form a circle; you become one.

I like to think that this book about my philosophy is just like a circle where the end, this final chapter, will flow into the beginning and then flow through the whole book toward the end. I began this little book by talking about God's plan and how we are all a part of God's plan, so now I want to tell you how my part in God's plan became clear to me.

Some people believe that God speaks to them through sacred writings, like the Bible or the Koran; other people go to their place of worship and let their priest, rabbi, or imam interpret the holy words for them. Some people meditate or spend long hours in prayer, believing that Buddha or Allah or whatever they call the Divinity, will speak to them in their minds. All of these ways are good, but I believe that God speaks to us through other people, so that is why I talk to everyone I meet. And I listen.

You may have noticed that as a child I spent much of my time observing and listening to the people around me. First it was my brothers and sister, then my parents, and of course, my Grandpop. I observed our servants, and the family that I lived with for a whole summer. Later I observed Mary and her daughters, and then, when I left home and went out on my own, I often stood on a street corner or sipped coffee in a café and looked at all the people around me. In almost every case, I could see something unique in each person that needed to be encouraged as well as something that needed to be fixed or changed. I saw what was good in them (and I believe that all people come into this world good!) and I saw what was broken or lacking.

As I said at the end of chapter fourteen, the hardest thing in the world to do is to change people, but then, you also know that I like a challenge, so why not choose a very big challenge? Why not choose to make changing people for the better the purpose of my life?

When I first thought this would be a good purpose for my life, I decided to take some courses in psychology. I happened to be in Cairo at the time where there are many fine universities, so I enrolled in one and took classes there for about two years. I didn't attend school full time because I have a restless nature and have always had difficulty sitting in a seat, listening to someone else talk. I am a man of action. For me, the ideal teacher would create classes that were more like the discussions held in my Daddy's living room when I was growing up, where one person would propose a thought, and then another would react or disagree, and the talk would move from person to person, always a different point of view and always engaging and stimulating. And, of course, I would have an opportunity to contribute to the discussion too.

Many years later, I found out that this kind of teaching is called the Socratic Method, named after a great philosopher, Socrates, who used to go every morning to a central place in his home city of Athens, Greece and wait for other people who liked to think and debate to show up. Sometimes they would sit there all day, each person contributing his thoughts on everything from local politics to the meaning of life. I would love to have been there.

But the classes at the universities in Cairo were very different from those of ancient Athens. First of all, usually only one person, the teacher, spoke during the class. Long reading assignments were given between each lecture, and in the lecture hall, you were supposed to take voluminous notes. Occasionally you were allowed to pose a question, but only to find out what the teacher thought. You could not question the validity of a psychological theory. You could not say, "I think something else about that!" The only way you could offer your own opinions was to write a paper, and even then, you had to support your theory with the words of other established authorities on the subject or carefully documented experiments. I listened, I observed, and sometimes I decided what these authorities were saying contained some truth, but I was also frustrated by psychological theories that tried to simplify all human behavior into a single pattern of thinking and motivation. It was as if all these great thinkers were trying to force all of the people of the world into a few basic uniforms. And I couldn't agree with that. Everyone is important, but everyone is different.

Now I am not saying that going to school isn't valuable; everyone can benefit from learning how other people have
165

done things. To learn every new skill on your own would be an incredible waste of time, but it is important also not to sit there like a brainless sponge and soak up the words and ideas of others. You must think about what you are told, and you must question it. And it is okay to say *I agree with this, but I don't agree with that* , especially when you are learning about what motivates people and what makes them successful and happy. You need to listen to everyone and you need to study your own heart as well. We are all unique in how we deal with life, but we are all the same in what we need and want.

One of my first attempts to change another human being occurred quite by accident. This also happened in Cairo, that ancient city where I lived off and on for several years, both attending school and working there. My very first employment was for a company based in Cairo that managed cruises for tourists on the Nile in large barges which were basically floating hotels. I liked that job because it gave me many opportunities to study people of all ages from all over the world, and then, when I wasn't working on a particular voyage, I could explore that busy city where so much human behavior happens on the street, right in front of your eyes, if you know how to look.

I was standing near an open-air market one day, watching the people, especially the tourists. A woman who was probably an American did an especially foolish thing at one stall. She knew enough to barter for the item she wished to buy, a lovely silk scarf, but she didn't know that she should never display a large amount of money in a public place. When she and the merchant agreed on the final price, she reached into the inside pocket of the light jacket she was wearing and pulled out a fat roll of currency. It was probably the equivalent of several hundred dollars

American, and this ignorant woman was unrolling the bundle and pulling off bills like they were worthless pieces of paper. She counted out the denominations into the shopkeeper's hand, stuffed the wad of money back into her jacket pocket, and took the parcel containing the scarf from him. Then she turned away and walked into the crowd.

A small woman dressed in the long dress and jihab typical of an ordinary Egyptian housewife was standing nearby; she was also watching this lady very carefully. As the tourist entered the crowd, the small woman walked toward her, looking off to her right like she wasn't paying attention to where she was going. The two women collided, they both offered apologies in their own languages, they smiled at each other, and then, each one walked away.

But I had been watching too. I had not actually seen the small hand of the Egyptian lady slip into the jacket of the tourist and remove the roll of bills; the thief had been very skillful and very quick! But I was certain that this had happened, and that the tourist was going to have considerable trouble getting back to her hotel and her companions when she discovered that she was now penniless on the streets of Cairo. I decided I wanted to help her.

I followed her down the street slowly and waited for her to stop moving. Finally she paused at another stall to examine some jewelry, so I walked over and stood a few feet away. "Excuse me, ma'am" I said in English with almost exaggerated courtesy, "but I think you should check to see if you still have all of your money."

The lady looked at me in alarm, but seeing that I wasn't

close enough to touch her, she reached inside her jacket as I had suggested. Her eyes opened wide in alarm, and she looked very frightened and confused. "How? When? I've been robbed!" she cried.

"Calm yourself, " I said. "Do not get upset, not here. What you need to do is to go back to your hotel right away. If you wish to make a report to the police, you should do it there. It would not be safe for you here in the market if you begin calling for the police like you would in the United States... and it wouldn't do any good. In fact, I think you must count this money as lost forever, but at least you have learned something. " At this point, I reached into my own wallet, which I always kept very close to my body, inside my shirt where I could feel it move if clever little fingers tried to grab it. I took out several bills which I handed to her.
"This should be enough to get you safely back to your hotel, " I said, and then, I walked with her to the edge of the bazaar and flagged down a taxi cab.

She thanked me profusely as she climbed in the cab, asking me how she could ever repay me, but I said there was no need. I told her she should never flash all her money in public like that. She should carry with her only what she really needed. And she should keep her money in a belt around her waist or the special envelope that many women put inside their bra. I watched her taxicab drive away and felt like I had done at least one person some good that day.

Now I was thirsty and was thinking about a cup of coffee, so I began walking toward my favorite cafe when I got that physical warning on the back of my neck, the prickle that tells you that someone is watching you. I spun around, and there, next to a nearby stall, was the thief. We stared at each other for a moment; then she greeted me politely in Egyptian Arabic. I nodded and returned her greeting.

"You saw?" she said.

"I didn't see, but I knew." I replied.

"Why didn't you grab me?" she said. "I think you could have. You are big and you are quick."

I looked at her kindly. "If I grabbed you and called the police, would this make your life better?" I asked.

"No," she said in alarm. "I would be thrown into jail!"

"Would you like to talk with me about this?" I went on. "We could go have some coffee."

"Okay," she said, and then she followed me down the narrow street, carefully walking several paces behind me. When we got to the cafe, I sat down and pulled out a chair for her. We both ordered Egyptian coffee, which is so strong and thick that you fear it will burn a hole in your stomach, even though you only get a little bit in the tiny cup.

When the waiter left to get our drinks, she spoke first. "I have always been a thief," she announced with a kind of bravado.

"How old were you when you first stole something?" I

169

looked at her calmly. It was very important that she knew I was interested in her life, but that I was not judging her. No one learns much from the judgment of others; in fact, when others point out our faults, we cling to these defects even more strongly in our own defense. We resist being *forced* to change. The desire to change must come from within because it is our judgment of ourselves that matters most.

"I was six, or maybe seven. My mother was a thief, and I learned from watching her."

"Where is your mother now?" I asked.

"She is dead. She died in prison. There was a riot one night in the prison, and the guards beat her to death, even though she wasn't taking part. She was just there."

"And your father?"

"I never knew him. When he took a new wife, she convinced him to get rid of me and my mother. You know..."

"Yes," I replied, "I know how that can happen." The waiter put our cups down and left. "So you live here near the bazaar and you make your own way? How old are you?"

"I am nineteen," she replied.

"And how many times have you gone to jail?" I asked.

"Only once," she answered with pride, "I am a very good thief."

I chuckled a little which made her smile. "Yes," I said, "I am sure you are a good thief."

I sipped some coffee and we sat in silence for a while. Then I spoke from my heart, "All people are good. No one is bad. We all do what we must to survive. I just wonder..." and then I looked at her beautiful hands which were lying on the table across from me, "if those clever fingers can't do something else to provide you with a living."

"I can stitch," she said. And then, she reached into one of the huge invisible pockets which Muslim women always have in the folds of their burkha and pulled out a small purse. It was made of black silk that was covered with fine needlework, colorful embroidery of leaves and flowers, and a small butterfly perched upon a stem. It was very delicate and must have taken some time.

"That is very nice," I said. "I don't think that every woman could do such fine work. I am sure you could sell such stitching to a merchant, or you might also find employment in a shop."

"I will think about it," she said as she drained her coffee cup and rose from the table.

"I wish you well," I replied. "Salaam alaikum."

For the next three weeks, I couldn't return to the bazaar because I was managing one of the tour barges which was headed down the Nile. It was usually my responsibility to live on and manage the barge which carried any children under the age of twelve. This way, they could have fun with other youngsters and their parents would be relieved of watching them during a good part of their trip. I liked working with the kids; they were far more easy to please than the adults, and I often found opportunities to talk with them and share my philosophy. By the end of the excursion, they were usually calling me Uncle Bazia.

But when that trip was over, I revisited the same market and was pleased when I finally spotted the lady thief. I could tell that something in her life had changed because she was standing up a little straighter, her head at a more confident angle. She didn't look like she was trying to be invisible anymore, and she was talking to a merchant at his stall. She was showing him a fabric belt covered with fine, colorful, embroidery, and he seemed to like it. When he handed her a few bills and took it from her, she smiled.

I didn't speak to her because this victory, this change in her life, was hers, not mine. I never saw her again.

One thing I am fond of saying about God's purpose is that it is bigger than you think. As I say this, I realize I am thinking back to the first chapter of this book where I explained to you that none of us can really see God's purpose, but that we are all a part of it, if we can only recognize the opportunities He creates for each of us when they arise. We humans often speak of coincidences, but I don't think there are any coincidences. I believe that each and every time something happens that makes us say, "Wow, isn't that strange?", we should be alert because it is very likely that God is offering us a chance to do good and move His plan ahead. Let me give you another example.

As I have told you, I love to talk, and in this age of the cell phone, I have ample opportunity to do so with people who are nearby as well as people who are on the other side of this planet. I always purchase unlimited cell phone use. In fact, I usually carry two cell phones because I don't ever want to be without this wonderful modern convenience. I often make or receive over two hundred phone calls a day! And believe it or not, this habit is how I have helped many people whom I have never met face to face, especially children.

This is how it happens; I make a lot of calls for business deals, to reach out to others in diaspora, and to talk with my friends. And what sometimes happens when I call is that the adult I wanted to speak to is not around, but a child answers the phone instead and politely tells me that Mommy or Daddy can't come to to the phone and that I should call back in a while. But I don't hang up. I think that children deserve the courtesy of being treated like people, so I always ask the child how he or she is and what's happening in the child's life. And the child begins to talk. It is as if the child has just been waiting for someone to ask, "How are you? Wha'sup?" I listen and I ask questions, and soon the child and I feel like we both have a new friend. When we are ready to stop talking, I ask the child if he (or she) would like to talk again sometime. The child always says, "Yes!" so I tell him to write down my number and to call me anytime. And I mean it.

If I don't hear from the child for a while, I call back myself, but that doesn't happen very often. It is as if there is a whole world of lonely children out there wanting someone to listen to them. Not all of the people I call or who call me

173

are children either; many are people I was told about by others, people whose lives have taken a very difficult turn and who need someone to talk to, or they may be people I met somewhere in a restaurant or on the street. I always give them my number. And we talk.

Talk is healing. I have said this many times and I thoroughly believe it. I know that if you go to a therapist or a psychiatrist, he will encourage you to talk about what is on your mind. But I am not sure that talking to someone for an hour a week or maybe two hours a month, a person you pay for this service, has the same effect as talking to someone who is slowly getting to know you and who is really listening because he cares. I also know that my philosophy gives me an unusual perspective on people's problems. I have traveled all over the world, I have listened to probably a million people, and I have a lot of common sense. And remember, I don't go by emotion. That means I don't judge them. I just listen.

I also don't encourage the people who talk to me to focus on events from the past which they believe have destroyed their happiness. I am actually kind of tough about that. You cannot change the past. Yes, sometimes you can learn something from it, but reliving the pain of the past over and over and over again accomplishes nothing. In fact, I believe it can do a great deal of harm because you feel like you are reliving your failures. It is best to move on as soon as you can.

Finally, I want to point out that I always tell the people who talk to me, whether they are children or adults, one thing: you don't have to like me and you don't have to agree with me. This fact about me is sometimes such a surprise to them that it is extremely liberating. More than once I have

174

been told that the person I was listening to and talking with was raised in a house where disagreement with their father or mother was severely punished. I am not talking about disobedience; that is something else. Children should obey their parents unless their parents are putting them or someone else in danger. I am talking about disagreement. If you are not allowed to hold opinions of your own, you become a little robot; you can't think for yourself; you cease to feel like a person. To end that terrible condition, you need to find the courage to say what you really think, out loud, and somebody has to be listening. And it is my opinion that listening is the most important thing I do.

A few years after I moved to the United States, I began seeking out some of the homeless people in our nation's capital. I lived in Pennsylvania, not far away, and so, when I had extra money and time off from work, I would drive to Washington, D.C., buy a large bag of hamburgers from a fast food chain, and take them to a park where many homeless men and women congregated. I had originally thought that Americans should be ashamed of the large numbers of homeless people living on their streets, especially in our beautiful capital, but after I talked to some of the social workers and police who were trying to change that situation, I learned that these vagrants had chosen this lifestyle, and that although their reasons, such as mental illness, alcoholism, and drug addiction, were often upsetting, they had a right to make this choice for themselves, and that there were many government agencies which provided them with the services they needed.

One day, I had just finished handing out the bags of burgers and was headed toward my car when I suddenly realized I had not spoken more than a brief hello to a single one of the people I had given food to. I had, for me, been quite cold and deliberate in my philanthropy, so I turned around and walked into the park again.

There was a man near the entrance sitting on a wrought iron bench. He was probably close to fifty. His hair was getting grey and his face was lined. He was wearing dirty clothes with many stains on them, but I could see that these garments had once been the pieces of an expensive Italian business suit. He also had on some very expensive shoes although they, too, were scuffed and stained. I was sure they needed new soles as well. His shirt collar was very frayed, but he was wearing a tie! He had a pile of shopping bags beside him, all of them stuffed with other clothes, blankets, and old newspapers. I decided to sit down next to him and ask him how he was.

At first I didn't think he heard me because he didn't respond and he didn't move, but I waited. Finally he turned and looked at me. "I have been sitting here, " the man said, "for seventeen years. And nobody has ever asked me how I was." He paused, took a deep breath, and then went on, "Do you really want to know?"

I replied that I did, that I always meant what I said, so he began to talk. He talked for over an hour. He told me the story of his life, of how he had been born and raised in the Midwest, grown up there like a lot of other people, gone off to Vietnam where he was briefly captured by the Vietcong and tortured, but then he was saved by a bunch of Green Berets. After that he was discharged from the military, came back to the States, got a free college education as a veteran, and finally became a stockbroker on Wall Street. There he had been a great success; he had made a great deal of money. He had married and had two children. But somehow, he never felt like his life had any meaning. He felt empty inside.

He began drinking heavily and this, of course, did not decrease his depression. His wife became very unhappy with him, and she filed for a divorce and moved away, taking their children with her. If anyone had really cared about him, they would have known that he needed a therapist; certainly if he had gone to one of the Veterans' Hospitals, they might have helped him. But he had been such a successful businessman that nobody could see what was happening until it was too late. They were looking at the uniform, not the man.

"I have been sitting here on this bench for seventeen years," he concluded, "just waiting for someone to ask me how I am. " At this point, he reached into the pocket of his shabby suitcoat and pulled out a large roll of bills. There were a few twenties on the top, but most of them were hundred dollar bills. He laid the stack on the bench between us and said, "That's about $3500." Then he pulled a ratty plaid blanket out of one of the bags. "There's at least another $10,000 in there, " he said, pointing to the bundles of neatly banded hundreds in the bottom of the bag. "Maybe more."

He leaned back, looked up at the sky, and smiled. "I have been waiting for you," he said. "And now I can get back to life."

I asked him if I could give him a ride anywhere, but he only smiled again and said, "No, I'll be fine now."

A few weeks later I returned to the park, but his bench was

empty. I wandered around, but there was no sign of the man. I returned several times over the next few months, but I never saw him again. I would like to think that when I sat down and asked him how he was, he decided to return to the land of the living. He certainly had the means, but did he have the motivation? I will never know.

One thing I do know from listening to the many people I have encountered in my travels around the world is that very few people believe in God anymore and even those who do don't believe in miracles. They go to their temple, mosque, or church on their special holy day each week, but when they go out the door, they leave their faith inside, like it was something separate from their day to day life. If someone were to ask them, are you a Christian or a Moslem or Jew or one of the other belief systems on this planet, they would answer; they often claim that their belief system is the best, but they rarely live as if they do. It's as if following your beliefs is somehow *not cool*. We are too bound up in what we call the real world; miracles, we say, only happen in old books, not in our real life of today.

One time a young girl whom I talked to regularly on my cell phone asked me a very difficult question. "What is the true religion, Bazia? Which one is right?"

I didn't even know at that time what she had been taught by her parents and I certainly didn't want to offend her or her family in any way, so I thought about it for a moment, and then, an answer came into my head.

"Imagine," I said, "that all the people in this world are living in a dark cave. We live and work and play and

178

interact in this cave, but in many ways, we are moving through the dark. Every now and then, a door opens into the cave and we glimpse a flash of light and sometimes we also see what is beyond the door, but then the door closes again, and we are back in the dark of our ignorance. Can you picture this?"

My young friend said she could, so I went on.

"From time to time in the history of our world, there are born people who know what is on the other side of the door. They remember it from before they were born. They don't remember it perfectly, but they remember parts of this wonderful place where everyone gets along and there is peace and love and unity. So as these people grow, they talk to others about the wonderful truth they remember. They are messengers. Buddha was such a messenger, and Jesus, and Mohammed, and Moses. And all of the prophets and saints and other people we look to for spiritual guidance. Do you understand?"

"Yes, I do," she said softly.

"So each of these messengers brings us different information and each one tries, in his own way, to lead us to the door. And as a result, when the messenger leaves this world, he leaves behind many people who believe in his wonderful truth."

"I think I understand, " she said.

179

"But here is something important," I continued. "You must respect and honor all of the messengers. You may have your own favorite because you understand his message and you feel comfortable with it, but the important parts of his message, trusting in God or Allah, doing good, and loving your fellow man, those are the same as all the other messengers. Only the words are different."

She told me that she liked my answer, that it made sense. And I said thank you to God because this was a new answer even for me, and I didn't believe that it was my answer. I believe it came from Him.

So now you know the most important way I try to follow God's plan in my life. I can summarize it best with this sentence: I use my greatest talent (which is my compassion for other people) to make the world a happier place, one person at a time. And although I don't always succeed, I don't stop trying. There is, for me, no greater satisfaction in this life.

My final comment to you is some advice. Please remember that you don't have to like me and you don't have to agree with me. But think about doing the same thing with your life. Find your greatest talent, whether it is creating music, programming a computer, giving comfort and relief to those in pain, making someone laugh, whatever it is, and use it to change the world. Join the circle.

22259933R00099

Made in the USA
Charleston, SC
16 September 2013